D0366707

Windows 2000 Commands
Pocket Reference

Windows 2000 Commands
Pocket Reference

Æleen Frisch

Beijing • Cambridge • Farnham • Köln • Paris • Sebastopol • Taipei • Tokyo

Windows 2000 Commands Pocket Reference

by Æleen Frisch

Copyright © 2001 O'Reilly & Associates, Inc. All rights reserved.
Printed in the United States of America.

Published by O'Reilly & Associates, Inc., 101 Morris Street,
Sebastopol, CA 95472.

Editor: Mike Loukides

Production Editor: Mary Sheehan

Cover Designer: Ellie Volckhausen

Printing History:

March 2001:   First Edition.

0-596-00148-7
[C]

Table of Contents

Windows 2000 Commands Pocket Reference

Introduction

This desktop reference documents Windows 2000 command mode. It is designed for system administrators, but will also prove beneficial to many other types of users. It includes most available Windows 2000 commands, as well as the most useful system administration command-line utilities from the Resource Kit (space permitting). Resource Kit commands are marked with an "RK" superscript in their header lines.

What's Not Included

Space limitations have forced us to exclude the following classes of special-purpose commands from this reference:

- Multiuser Terminal Services commands (since this facility is an add-on to the standard Windows 2000 products)
- Clustering-related utilities
- Most NetWare-related commands and options
- SNMP-related commands
- Multicast networking–related commands
- Services for Macintosh commands
- Java subsystem–related commands

A few additional commands are also excluded, either because they have been deemed redundant, obscure, obsolete, broken, unacceptably insecure, or because they perform inadvisable actions or procedures. Lingering unneeded DOS commands (e.g., **subst**, commands used in Config.SYS files, etc.) are likewise omitted.

Finally, whenever several utilities perform essentially identical tasks, only the best of them are included.

Organization

Commands are arranged in groups related to their purposes and functions; within a group, commands are arranged alphabetically. Consult the index to locate a desired command. Command options are grouped by function and ordered by importance. Occasionally, unimportant options are omitted.

Much of the information in this book not only corresponds to Windows 2000, but also applies to earlier versions of Windows NT. Some commands are available only with the Server or Advanced Server version of the operating system.

Typographic Conventions

cmd
> Bold denotes a Windows 2000 command or option.

arg
> Italics denotes variable parameters (i.e., things you must fill in).

[...]
> Brackets denote optional parts of commands.

a | b
> A pipe indicates that either *a* or *b* should be selected.

cmdRK
> The "RK" superscript denotes a Resource Kit command.

HKLM

HKCU

Registry key initial components are abbreviated.

Menu name→menu name . . .

The arrow symbol (→) combined with boldface denotes a Windows 2000 menu path.

Entering Commands

- Commands are not case-sensitive.

- Command options are not usually case-sensitive. The few options that are lowercase only are specified as such in this book. Uppercase and mixed-case options can be assumed to be case-insensitive.

- Command options are generally preceded by a forward slash—for example, **/X**. In many cases, a minus sign may be substituted for the slash if desired. A few commands (mostly originating in the Resource Kit) require that their options be preceded by a minus sign.

- Option placement is not consistent across all commands. Consult the syntax summary for option placement for a specific command.

- Distinct command arguments are separated by spaces, commas, or semicolons.

- A command may be continued onto a second (or subsequent) line by placing a caret (^) as the final character of the initial line.

- The caret is also used as the escape symbol, protecting the following character from being processed by the command interpreter.

- Multiple commands may be concatenated by an ampersand: *command1* **&** *command2*. The commands are executed in sequence.

- Commands may be executed conditionally, based on the success or failure of a preceding command, by joining them with **&&** or | | (respectively):

command1 **&&** *command2*
> Execute *command2* only if *command1* succeeds.

command1 | | *command2*
> Execute *command2* only if *command1* fails.

I/O Redirection

< *file*
> Take standard input from a file.

> *file*
1> *file*
> Send standard output to a file.

>> *file*
1>> *file*
> Append standard output to a file.

2> *file*
> Send standard error to a file.

2>> *file*
> Append standard error to a file.

> *file 2>&1*
> Combine standard output and standard error and send both to the same destination (use >> before *file* to append).

command1 | *command2*
command1 0> *command2*
> Form a pipe, linking the standard output of *command1* to the standard input of *command2*.

Environment Variables

This section lists several key Windows 2000 environment variables. Note that environment variables are dereferenced by enclosing the name between percent signs—for example, %SystemRoot%. System and current user environment variables are modified via the path **My Computer Properties→Advanced→Environment Variables**:

PATH
> A semicolon-separated list of directories, which are searched in turn for a command entered without a full path.

PATHEXT
> A semicolon-separated list of file extensions that should be applied in turn to bare command names when searching for the proper executable. Extensions in the list must include the initial period.

PROGRAMFILES
> The location of the Program Files folder (usually C:\Program Files).

SYSTEMROOT
> The location of the Windows 2000 system directory (usually C:\WinNT).

TEMP and TMP
> Paths to a directory that applications may use for temporary file and scratch storage space.

Installing Extra Administrative Commands

The Windows 2000 distribution CD includes several additional groups of administrative commands that must be installed separately. They are in the following directory locations on the CD:

- \Support\Tools\Setup: this installs tools into %SystemRoot%\Program Files\Support Tools

- \Support\Tools\Deploy.Cab: this contains system installation automation tools; these must be installed manually to whatever location you desire

- \I386\AdminPak.MSI: this installs tools into a standard system software tree (i.e., under %SystemRoot%)

- \ValueAdd\3rdParty\Mgmt\Winstel\SwiAdmLE.MSI: this installs tools into %SystemRoot%\Program Files\VERITAS Software

The Resource Kit must be purchased separately (available from most booksellers and software sellers). Once installed, these tools are located in the directory %SystemRoot%\Program Files\Resource Kit. Note that a few tools must be installed manually; they are generally located in subdirectories of \Apps on the Resource Kit CD.

Help Commands

help *command*
> Obtain help for a standard Windows 2000 command.

command **/?**
> Obtain help for the specified command.

net help *command*
> Obtain help for one of the net commands.

net helpmsg *nnnn*
> Explain Windows 2000 message number *nnnn*.

ntbooks
> Open main Windows 2000 help file. Navigate to **Troubleshooting and Additional Resources→Additional Resources→Windows 2000 Commands** in the help file to find documentation of the various commands.

W2RKSupp.Chm
> The help file for the additional support tools available on the Windows 2000 distribution CD.

Deploy.Chm and Unattend.Doc
> The help files and documentation related to unattended and other automated Windows 2000 installations (these files are located wherever you installed the installation

automation tools from the Windows 2000 distribution CD, discussed in the previous section).

W2RKTool.Chm[RK]

The main help file for Resource Kit commands. Other useful help files in the Resource Kit include:

- W2RKBook.Chm[RK]: Resource Kit books.

- RegEntry.Chm[RK]: Descriptions of registry keys and values.

- GP.Chm[RK]: Descriptions of many Group Policy settings.

- W2000Msgs.Chm[RK]: Documentation of Windows 2000 error messages and event log entry types.

- Counters.Chm[RK]: Documentation of all Performance Monitor counters.

General-Purpose Commands

---

clip[RK]

command | **clip**
clip < *file*

Place the command output file /specified file contents on the system clipboard.

---

cmd

cmd [*options*] [**/C** | **/K** [**/S**] *command*]

Start a new Windows 2000 command interpreter. If *command* is specified, that command is executed. Enclose multiple commands in quotation marks. See the **cmd /?** documentation for other features (e.g., command/path completion, delayed environment variable expansion, and so on).

Use the **exit** command to end a command interpreter session.

Options

/C | **/K** [**/S**]

Carry out the specified command, retaining (**/C**) or terminating (**/K**) the command interpreter afterward. With either **/C** or **/K**, **/S** says to process quotes in the command string before execution. (Usually they are preserved.)

/Q

Disable command echoing (see **echo OFF**, later in this book).

/E:ON | **OFF**

Enable/disable command interpreter extensions. Set the default by the value of the HKCU\ or HKLM\ Software\Microsoft\Command Processor\Enable Extensions registry key (enabled by default).

/A | **/U**

Format command output as ANSI (default) or Unicode, respectively.

/D

Disable registry autorun commands in the HKLM\ or HKCU\Software\Microsoft\Command Processor\Autorun registry key.

---

cscript

cscript [*script*] [*options*]

Run a script using the Windows Scripting Host facility. The script filename must include a recognized extension indicating the scripting language. See the **ntbooks** documentation for script execution–related options. Note that **cscript** options are preceded by two slashes (//) in order to distinguish them from the script's own options.

cscript //h:cscript

Make **cscript** the default script host, which allows scripts to be run by entering the script name as the command.

---

date

date [*mm-dd*-[*yy*]*yy*] [**/T**]

Set to the specified date (prompted if omitted). The **/T** option displays the date without modifying it.

---

doskey

doskey [*options*]

Recall previous commands or create macros (aliases).

Command History and Editing Options
/HISTORY
Display the entire command history list.

/LISTSIZE=*n*
Set the size of the history list to *n*.

Once **doskey** is loaded, press F7 to display a selectable command history list, press Alt-F7 to clear it, and press F9 to go to a specific command number.

/INSERT | /OVERSTRIKE
Set the default editing mode for recalled commands to insert or overstrike (generally the default).

Macro Options

macroname=command
Define a macro. Within *command*, **$T** inserts a command separator, **$1** through **$9** denote command arguments one through nine, and **$*** denotes all command arguments.

/MACROS:ALL
Display all defined macros.

/MACROFILE=*file*
Install all macros stored in the specified file.

/EXENAME=*exefile*
Specify an executable file to associate with the macros being defined.

/MACROS:*exefile*
Display all defined macros associated with the specified executable file.

The Alt-F10 key sequence clears all defined macros.

---

find

find [*options*] *string* [*files*]

Search for a literal text string in the specified files, in standard input (via a pipe), or in text entered at its prompt, and display matching lines.

Options

/V

> Display only nonmatching lines.

/I

> Perform a case-insensitive search (case-sensitive is the default).

/C

> Display a count of matching lines only.

/N

> Display the line number preceding each line.

---

findstr

findstr [*options*] **/C:**string | **/G:**file | strings [files]

Search for one or more text strings or regular expressions in the specified files or in standard input (if no files are given), and display matching lines. Enclose multiple search strings in quotation marks.

Options

/R

> Interpret search strings as regular expressions.

/L

> Interpret search strings as literal text.

/C:string

> Designate the specified string as a literal text string (useful for strings with internal spaces).

/G:file

> Read the search strings from the specified file. A slash for *file* says to read the filename from the console.

/B | **/E**

> Match the search string only at the beginning (**/B**) or end (**/E**) of a line (don't include both).

/I

> Perform a case-insensitive search.

/V

> Display nonmatching lines.

/X

> Display only lines that match exactly.

/N | **/O**

> Precede displayed lines with their line numbers or character offsets, respectively.

/M
>Display only the names of files containing a match.

/S
>Recurse subdirectories in the file list.

/F:*file*
>Read the file list from the specified file. A slash for *file* says to read the file list from the console.

/D:*dirlist*
>Search the files in the comma-separated directory list.

/P
>Skip files containing nonprintable characters.

Regular Expression Components

.
>Any single character.

^ $
>Beginning/end of line.

\< | \>
>Beginning/end of word.

x
>Literal character: used to escape special characters in regular expressions (e.g., **\$** refers to a literal dollar sign).

[*chars*]
>Any character in the list.

[^*chars*]
>Any character not in the list.

[*a–z*]
>Any character falling in the indicated character range. Note that multiple ranges and character lists can be placed inside a single set of brackets.

*
>Zero or more of the previous item; e.g., [0–9]* means zero or more numbers and .* means zero or more characters (matches anything).

---

logoff^{RK}

logoff /F /N

End the current logon session, suppressing all confirmation prompts.

---

more

more [*options*] [*files*]

Display its standard input or the contents of the specified files, one screen at a time.

Options

/C

Clear the screen before displaying the first page.

/S

Combine (squeeze) multiple blank lines into one.

/T*n*

Expand tabs to *n* spaces. By default, tabs are expanded to eight spaces.

/P

Expand form feed characters.

+*n*

Begin the display at line *n* of the input or first file.

The command also uses any options set in the MORE environment variable.

---

now^{RK}

now *string*

Precede the specified string with the current date and time (designed to create timestamped message strings).

---

path

path [*path*]

Display or set the search path (a semicolon-separated list of directories). The form %path% may be used to include the current search path in a modified one.

---

pathman^{RK}

pathman /*option path*

Manipulate the user or system PATH variables according to the specified option. The latter is in the form /*xy*, where *x* is **a** (add the specified path components) or **r** (remove components) and *y* is **u** (user path) or **s** (system path).

---

qgrep^{RK}

qgrep [*options*] *regular-expressions files*
Search files for patterns and display matching lines.

Options

/B | /E
 Match pattern at the beginning/end of a line.

/L | /X
 Treat search strings as literal/regular expressions. **/X** is the default.

/V | /X
 Display nonmatching/exactly matching lines.

/Y
 Perform a case-insensitive search.

/N
 Precede displayed lines with line numbers.

/L
 Display the filename only if the file contains a match.

---

setx^{RK}

setx *env-variable value* [*-m*]
Set the value of an environment variable in the current user or computer (**–m**) environment (as if you had used the **My Computer→Properties→Advanced→Environment Variables** dialog). **setx** also has more complex variations; see W2RKTools.Chm for details.

---

sort

sort [*options*] [*< file*]
Sort standard input (use I/O redirection to sort a file).

Options

/R
 Reverse usual sort order (i.e., Z to A, 9 to 0).

/+*n*
 Start sorting in column *n*.

/L C

Sort according to characters' binary encodings rather than the sort order implied by the system default locale.

/REC *n*

Specify the maximum number of characters (*n*) per line. The default is 4,096 and the maximum value is 65,535.

/T *path*

Use the indicated directory as the command's temporary working directory. The default is the system temporary directory.

/O *output-file-path*

Write the sorted data to the specified file rather than as standard output.

---

time

time *[hr[:min[:sec[.hd]]]]* **[A | P] [/T]**

Set the time (prompted if omitted). The **/T** option displays the time without modifying it.

---

title

title *string*

Set the title of the current command (cmd.exe) window.

---

ver

ver

Display the Windows 2000 operating system version.

---

where[RK]

where *[/r dir] filename*

Display the full path to the specified file, searching the current search path (default) or the directory tree that is rooted at the indicated directory.

Options

/t
> Display the sizes and times for all located files.

/e
> Display the executable type of each located file.

---

whoami[RK]

whoami

Display the username of the currently logged-in user.

Options

/User
> Display username (required if this information is desired along with additional options).

/Groups
> Display group memberships.

/Priv
> Display user rights.

/SID
> Display SIDs along with other information (can't be used alone).

/All
> Display entire security access token.

General Administrative Commands

---

assoc

assoc [.*ext=filestypename*]

Associate a file extension with a named file type. See also **ftype**.

---

ftype[RK]

ftype [*filetypename=command-string*]

Display (no parameters) or define file type–specific command invocations. In the latter mode, the specified command is invoked whenever a file of the specified type is executed. See also **assoc**.

---

mode

```
mode COMn:  BAUD=b  PARITY=p  DATA=d  STOP=s  ^
    xon=on | off  to=on | off  odsr=on | off  octs=on |  ^
    off  rts=on | off | hs | tg  idsr=on | off  dtr=on |  ^
    off | hs
```

Set the characteristics of a serial line. See the **ntbooks** documentation for details about the available settings as well as other forms of this command.

msinfo32

MSInfo32 /Report *file* [**/Computer** *name*]

Create a report of the system configuration for the local or specified system and place it in the specified text file. See W2RKSupp.Chm for options to limit the output and change its format. Note that similar functionality is provided by the graphical utility **winrep**.

This command is located in the %ProgramFiles%\Common Files\Microsoft Shared\MSInfo directory (this directory is not typically in the PATH).

net computer

net computer *host* **/ADD** | **/DELETE**

Add or remove the specified computer from the domain database.

net name

net name [*name*] [**/DELETE**]

Without parameters, display the current name set (message recipients targeted to this user account). If an argument is included, the command adds the specified name to the current name set.

The **/DELETE** option removes the specified name from the name set.

net send

net send *who message*

Send a message to one or more users. *who* may be one of the following:

- A username
- A message recipient defined with **net name**
- A hostname (corresponds to any user logged into the specified computer)
- An asterisk for all users in the local domain
- **/DOMAIN:***name* for all users in the specified domain
- **/USERS** for all users with connections to the local server

---

net time

```
net time from [/SET]
```

Display the system time on a specified system. **/SET** says to synchronize the local time with it. *from* takes the form *hostname*, **/DOMAIN:***name*, or **/RTSDOMAIN:***name*; the latter specifies the domain of a Reliable Time Server.

```
net time [\\host] [/QUERYSNTP | /SETSNTP:servers]
```

Display or set the name of the Network Time Protocol (NTP) server(s) used by the local or specified system. The server list in the **/SETSNTP** option is space-separated.

---

shutdown[RK]

```
shutdown \\remote-host | /L [options] [message]
```

Shut down a Windows 2000 system. Include **/L** to shut down the local system or to specify a remote host as the command's first argument.

Options

/R

  Reboot after shutting down.

/T:*n*

  Wait *n* seconds before shutting down (the default is 20).

/Y

  Answer yes to all subsequent prompts.

/A

  Abort a pending shutdown.

/C

  Close open applications without saving data.

---

timezone[RK]

timezone /G | **/S** *start-date end-date*

Display (**/G**) or set (**/S**) the starting and ending dates for the current time zone's daylight savings time.

uptime[RK]

uptime [*server*]

Display the amount of time since the last boot for the local or specified system.

Working with Files

attrib

attrib [*options*] [*files*]

Set DOS file attributes (or display the current attributes if no options are specified). The file list defaults to all files in the current directory.

Options

+x | *−x*

Add or remove an attribute, where *x* is one of the following code characters: **R** (read-only), **H** (hidden), **S** (system) or **A** (archive).

/S

Recurse subdirectories in the file list.

/D

Apply attributes to folders themselves.

cacls, xcacls[RK]

cacls | **xcacls** *files* [*options*]

Display (if no options are specified) or modify access control lists (ACLs), using Windows NT 4 or Windows 2000 permission sets, respectively.

Options

Multiple options and instances of options are allowed.

/T

    Propagate changes to subdirectories in the file list.

/E

    Edit the existing ACL (the default is to replace it).

/G *user:perms*[*;dir-perms*]
/P *user:perms*[*;dir-perms*]

    Grant or replace (respectively) permissions in the access control entries (ACEs) for the specified user. *perms* indicates the defined permission set. For **cacls**, it is either **R** (read), **C** (change), **F** (full control), or **N** (none, applies to **/P** with **cacls** only). **xcacls** uses several additional codes for the other atomic permissions: **P** (change permissions), **O** (take ownership), **X** (execute), **W** (write), and **D** (delete). Directories take a second permission string, separated from the first by a semicolon. In this context, there is an additional code letter: **T** (not specified).

/R *user*

    Remove the ACEs for the specified user (requires **/E**).

/D *user*

    Deny the specified user all access to the files.

/C

    Continue applying changes even if an error occurs.

/Y

    Suppress confirmation prompts (**xcacls** only).

---

comp

comp [*options*] *fileset1 fileset2*

Compare two sets of files (or individual files). If multiple files are specified, compare files of the same name. Differences are reported only for files of identical size. (Use **fc** to compare files of different sizes.)

Options

/A

    Display the differences in ASCII form (the default is decimal).

/L

    Display line numbers for differing lines.

/C

    Perform a case-insensitive comparison.

/N=n

    Compare only the first n lines of each file.

---

compact

compact [*options*] [*files*]

Compress or uncompress the specified files, setting directories' default settings, or display the compression status of the specified files. If omitted, the file list defaults to the current directory and its contents.

Options

/C | /U

Specify a compression operation or an uncompression operation, respectively.

/S[:*dir*]

Recurse subdirectories in the file list. If specified, *dir* sets the current working directory.

/F

Force compression even on already compressed files. (These are skipped by default.)

/I

Continue processing files even if an error occurs.

/Q

Request terse output.

/A

Display hidden and system files that are omitted by default (these files are processed, however).

convert

convert *x*: **/FS:NTFS**

Convert Drive *x* to an NTFS filesystem. Add the **/V** option for more verbose output.

copy

copy [*options*] *source destination*

Copy files to *destination*. If *destination* is a single file, all *source* files are concatenated. (The form *file1* + *file2* + ... may also be used to specify file concatenation.)

Options

/A | /B

Designate an ASCII or binary file, respectively (precedes source filenames and follows destination filename).

/V

Verify the copied data after writing.

/N

Use 8.3 filenames for the copied files.

/Z

Perform a restartable network file copy operation.

/Y | /-Y

Suppress/require confirmation of file overwrites, respectively.

---

del

del [*options*] *files*

Delete files. **erase** is a synonym for **del**.

Options

/S

Recurse subdirectories in the file list.

/Q

Suppress all confirmation prompts.

/P

Confirm every deletion operation.

/F

Force deletion of read-only files.

/A:*codes*

Select only files with specified attributes: **H** for hidden, **S** for system, **R** for read-only, and **A** for archive.

---

dir

dir [*options*] [*path*]

Display directory contents. *path* defaults to the current directory.

Options

Options may be set in the DIRCMD environment variable, and may be overridden by including the option on the command line, preceded by a minus sign (e.g., **/–N**).

/B

Display filenames only, one per line (omit the header line).

/W | /D

Wide directory listing: display several filenames per output line, ordering them by row or column, respectively.

/Q

Display file owners.

/N

Display Unix-style long directory listing (filenames appear on the right).

/L

Display all filenames in lowercase.

/X

Show 8.3 filenames in addition to long filenames.

/S

Recurse subdirectories.

/O:*sort-order*

Specify ordering of displayed files, using the following codes: **N** (by name), **E** (by extension), **S** (by size), **D** (date and time), and **G** (list directories first). To reverse the usual sort order, precede any code letter with a minus sign .

/T:*timecode*

Select which time to display and use for sorting: **C** (creation time), **A** (access time), or **W** (modification time, which is the default).

/A:*codes*

Select only files with specified attributes: **D** for directories, **H** for hidden, **S** for system, **R** for read-only, and **A** for archive. A minus sign before a code letter indicates that files of that particular type are to be excluded.

/C | /–C

Include/omit commas from file sizes. (The default is to include them.)

/4

Display years in four digits.

/P

Pause after each output screen.

---

fc

fc [*options*] *fileset1 fileset2*

Compare files or sets of files, displaying the differences between them. If multiple source files are specified, files of the same name in the second file set are compared.

Options

/B | **/L** | **/U**

Compare the files as binary files, ASCII text files, or Unicode text files, respectively. No other options can be combined with **/B**.

/C

Perform a case-insensitive comparison.

/W

Compress all whitespace before comparing.

/T

Don't expand tabs to spaces.

/LB*n*

Specify the maximum number of consecutive mismatches.

/*n*

Specify the number of consecutive matching lines required after a mismatch before the files are considered synchronized once again. (The default is 2.)

/A

Limit the display to just the first and final lines of each set of differences.

/N

Include line numbers in the display. (Valid for text files only.)

filever

filever [*options*] *file(s)*

Display the available version information for the specified file(s).

Options

/S

Recurse subdirectories.

/B

Bare format; exclude the header line for each file.

/V

Verbose output.

/A /D

Suppress file attributes (**/A**) or date and time (**/D**) from the listing.

/E

List only executable files in the display (e.g., .EXE, .DLL, etc.).

---

inuse^RK

inuse *replace-file drive:\path\target-file* [*/Y*]

Replace a locked file. Both file specifications must consist of full pathnames; the replacement file may be specified by the physical or UNC path. **/Y** suppresses the confirmation prompt.

---

linkd^RK

linkd *location target* | **/D**

Manipulate the junction (symbolic link) at the specified *location* (an empty folder). Specifying *target* creates a new junction pointing to that folder or device, and specifying **/D** removes an existing junction.

---

mcopy^RK, mtc^RK

mcopy *log-file source-file destination-file*
mtc *log-file source-dir destination-dir*

Perform a logged copy operation, either for an individual file or for a directory tree. The operation log is written to the file specified as the first command argument.

---

move

move [**/Y**] *files destination*

Move files to new directory location. Use **/Y** to suppress overwrite confirmation prompts.

---

net file

net file [*id* [**/CLOSE**]]

Without arguments, list all open shared files and their ID numbers. When an *id* is specified, information about that item is displayed and the **/CLOSE** option closes the file.

---

ntbackup backup [**systemstate**] *bksfile* **/J** *jobname* [*options*]

Perform the backup operation specified in the backup selection file (*bksfile*), assigning the job the specified job name. The .BKS file must be created beforehand, using the command's graphical interface.

If **systemstate** is included, system-related databases and files are also backed up (for example, registry, Active Directory databases, SYSVOL, and so on).

Note that restore operations can only be performed via the GUI version of this utility. For **systemstate** restores, see **ntdsutil**.

Options

Only one of the three following option sets may be selected:

/A /G *guid* | **/T** *tapename*
Append the backup set to the specified tape. (The default is to replace its current data.) Use either **/G** or **/T** to specify the destination (by GUID or tape name, respectively).

/P *poolname* **/UM**
Specify the media pool to use as the backup destination. The backup command finds the first available media of the specified type, then formats it and uses it for the backup operation.

/F *filename*
Specify the destination for a backup to a file.

The options specified in the .BKS file serve as defaults for the backup operation. The following command-line options can be used to override those settings:

/V:YES | **NO**
Verify/don't verify the backup after writing it.

/HC:ON | **OFF**
Specify the hardware compression setting.

/N *name*
Specify the media name. Invalid with **/A**.

/D *set-label*
Specify the backup set label.

/M *type*
Select the backup type, which can be normal, copy, incremental, differential, or daily.

/R:YES | **NO**
Restrict/don't restrict the backup set to the owner and members of the Administrators group.

/L: *type*
> Specify the log file type for the backup operation, either **f** (full), **s** (summary), or **n** (none).

/RS:YES | NO
> Backup/exclude the removable storage database.

/DS *server*
> Back up the Exchange directory service file on the specified server.

/IS *server*
> Back up the Exchange information store file on the specified server.

---

ntdsutil

ntdsutil

This command must be run after a system state restore operation is completed in order to authoritatively restore the Active Directory data. (It is required when restoring database files that have been replicated to other DCs.) Once **ntdsutil** completes, the system should be rebooted.

---

oh^{RK}

oh [*options*]

Display open handles.

Options

/P *pid*
> Limit display to handles associated with the specified process.

/T *type*
> Limit display to handles of the specified type.

string
> Limit display to handles whose name contains the specified string.

/A
> Include unnamed objects.

Note that when multiple options are specified, only handles matching all of them are displayed.

pax

pax [*options*] [*path*]

POSIX-compatible archive/backup program, capable of reading **tar** (the default) and **cpio** (use **–x cpio**) archives on disk.

pax –f *archive*

List the contents of the specified archive.

pax –r –f *archive* [**–s** *replace-cmd*] [*pattern-list*]

Extract the contents of the specified archive to the current directory, limiting extracted items to those matching a pattern in the list (if specified). The **–s** option says to perform the sed-style replacement command on each incoming filename.

pax –w [**–a**] **–f** *archive* [**–s** *replace-cmd*] [*paths*]

Create the specified archive, placing the indicated files and subtrees within it. If **–a** is included, then the archive is appended to, rather than replaced.

See the **ntbooks** documentation for additional operating modes and options.

---

permcopy^{RK}

permcopy *server share* *dest-server share*

Copy permission from the specified server and share to the destination server and share.

---

perms^{RK}

perms [*options*] *user files*

Display the specified user's permissions for the specified files.

Options

/S

    Recurse subdirectories.

/I

    Display permissions corresponding to interactive access.

---

ren

ren *path new-name*

Rename the specified file. **rename** is a synonym for **ren**.

replace

replace *source-files destination* [*options*]

Replace/update files in a destination directory.

Options

/A
> Add new files to the destination directory. This is not valid with **/U** or **/S**.

/U
> Update only destination files that are older than their corresponding source files.

/S
> Recurse subdirectories.

/R
> Replace read-only files.

/P
> Require confirmation for all replacements and additions.

rsdiag

rsdiag [*options*]

Display information in or from Remote Storage facility databases.

Options

/S | **/V** | **/M**
> Display storage media/volume/manageable volume lists. **/V** also optionally accepts a drive letter in order to obtain detailed information about that volume.

/W *full-path*
> Display the physical storage media and data set storing the most recent version of the specified file.

/J [*jobname*]
> List all pending jobs or detailed information about the specified job.

/C *jobname*

    Cancel the specified job.

/R [**/F**]

    Display contents of the recall queue. **/F** requests more detailed data.

/X *recallnum*

    Cancel a pending recall operation.

/I

    Display version information for the database files.

/T

    Reload trace files.

/D *type full-path*

    Write database information to the specified file. *type* indicates the desired data: **e** (Engine database), **f** (File System Agent database), **a** (File System Agent collection), **n** (Engine collection), or **s** (Subsystem collection).

---

rsdir

rsdir *item* [*options*]

Display information about Remote Storage facility status for the specified items (i.e., whether or not they are offline).

Options

/S

    Recurse subdirectories.

/F

    Display extended file information.

---

srvcheck^{RK}

srvcheck *host*

List all shares and their access permissions on the specified computer system.

---

subinacl^{RK}

subinacl [**/Test_Mode**] */type items /action*

Modify ACLs for the specified items. **/Test_Mode** says to indicate the action to take, but not actually to perform it. This command cannot be used on Dfs volumes.

/Type indicates the items' object type: **/file**, **/share**, **/subdirectories** (traverse directory tree), **/keyreg** and **subkeyreg** (registry keys, with or without recursion), **/service**, **/printer**, and **/kernelobject**.

Actions are options that specify a transformation of the existing ACL (the default action is to display the ACL). Here are some of the most useful (see W2RKTools.Chm for a full list):

/Owner=_User_
> Set item ownership.

/Replace=_Old-user_**=**_New-user_
> Reassign the ACEs from the old user to the new user.

/ChangeDomain=_Old-domain_**=**_New-domain_
> Replace all ACEs from the old domain with the corresponding ones from the new domain. There must be a trust relationship between the two domains.

/MigrateDomain=_Old-domain_**=**_New-domain_
> Copy all ACEs from the old domain, changing them to the corresponding ACEs from the new domain. There must be a trust relationship between the two domains.

/Grant=_Name_**=**_Perms_
/Deny=_Name_**=**_Perms_
> Add a grant/denial ACE for the specified user or group, having the specified permissions. (See W2RKTools.Chm for permission codes.)

---

takeown^{RK}

takeown *files*

Take ownership of system-owned files.

---

type

type *file*

Display file contents.

---

xcopy

xcopy *files destination* [*options*]

Copy directory trees.

Options

/EXCLUDE:*file*

Exclude all files matching any of the patterns listed in the specified file (one per line) from the copy operation.

/R

Overwrite read-only files.

/U

Update mode. Copy only files that already exist in the destination directory tree.

/D:*m-d-y*

Copy only files modified on or after the specified date.

/A | **/M**

Select files with the archive attribute set, then leave it set or unset, respectively.

/H

Include hidden and system files.

/S

Recurse nonempty subdirectories.

/T

Reproduce the directory tree structure but don't copy any files (excludes empty subdirectories).

/E

Include empty directories (implies **/S**, unless used with **/T**).

/V

Verify the copied data.

/I

Force the destination to be interpreted as a directory.

/Q | **/F**

Produce terse or verbose output, respectively.

/L

List files to be copied by the command, but don't actually copy any files.

/P

Require confirmation for each destination file.

/K

Reproduce the read-only status of copied files.

/N

Copy using 8.3 filenames.

/C

Continue copying even if an error occurs.

/Z

Copy network files in a restartable operation.

/Y

Suppress overwrite confirmation prompts.

/W

Prompt before beginning copy operation.

Working with Directories

append

append *path-list* [*options*]

Create a search path of directories for datafiles (used in addition to the current folder), where *path-list* is a semicolon-separated list of directories (use a single semicolon to clear the append path).

Options

/X[:on | off]

Turn use of the append path on or off. In order to use this option, the first **append** command executed must include **/X:on**. **on** is the default if no setting is given to **/X**.

/Path[:on | off]

Specify whether to search the append path for datafiles including full paths. The default is **on**.

/E

Set the value of the APPEND environment variable to the **append** path, allowing it to be viewed subsequently with **set**.

cd

cd [**/D**] [*path*]

Display or set the current working directory. If *path* does not include a drive letter, the current drive is assumed. Use **/D** to change to the current directory on the specified drive when it is different from the current drive. (The default is to just set it.) The form .. is used to refer to a parent directory.

chdir is a synonym for **cd**.

cipher

cipher [*options*] [*paths*]

Display encryption status (default operation) or encrypt/decrypt files. The list of paths defaults to the current directory. The options **/E** and **/D** specify encryption or decryption. (The default mode is a status display.)

cipher /E | **/D** *dirs*

Mark specified folders as encrypted/decrypted (affecting subsequently added files).

cipher /E | **/D /S:***dir*

Mark all folders in the specified directory subtree.

cipher /E | **/D /A** *specs*
cipher /E | **/D /A /S:***dir specs*

Encrypt/decrypt all files and mark all subdirectories matching the wildcard specifications in the current directory (first form), or throughout the directory tree, beginning at the specified directory. Omit *specs* in the second form to operate on an entire subtree.

Additional Options

/I
> Continue on error.

/H
> Include system and hidden files.

/F
> Force encryption/decryption of all items, regardless of their current status.

/Q
> Quiet mode.

delrp[RK]

delrp *path*

Delete the specified item, along with any associated reparse points.

diruse[RK]

diruse [/*] [*dirs*]

Compute and display disk space usage by directory for the specified directories (or the top-level folders within the specified directories, if the option is included).

Options

/S

  Give subtotals for each subfolder.

/M | /K

  Display totals in megabytes or kilobytes (bytes is the default).

/C

  Use the compressed file size rather than the apparent file size.

/Q:*n* [/A] [/D] [/O]

  Mark folders exceeding the specified size with **!** in the output (*n* has the same units as the output). **/A** also generates an alert, **/D** limits the display to folders greater than the specified size, and **/O** checks only the total sizes of the specified directories, rather than also checking all subfolders beneath them.

/,

  Place commas in numbers greater than 999 in the output.

---

efsinfo[RK]

efsinfo [*path* | /S:*dir*]

Display encrypted file/folder information. By default, the command lists the status of the items in the current or specified directory, or in the subdirectory tree specified to **/S**.

Options

[/R] | [/C]

  Display recovery agent/certificate thumbnail information for each item, respectively.

/Y

  Display the current EFS certificate thumbnail for the local computer, if accessible.

/I

  Continue on error.

---

md

md *path*

Create a directory (and all missing intermediates). **mkdir** is a synonym for **md**.

popd

popd

Return to the directory at the top of the directory stack (and remove it from the stack).

pushd

pushd [*path*]

Change the current working directory to the specified directory, and save the previous location in a directory stack (return with **popd**). Without an argument, **pushd** displays the current directory stack.

rd

rd [*options*] *path*

Remove a subdirectory. **rmdir** is a synonym for **rd**.

Options

/S
> Remove the entire subtree.

/Q
> Suppress confirmation prompts.

sfc

sfc [*options*]

Replace incorrect versions of system files with canonical versions.

Options

/ScanNow | **/PurgeCache** | **/ScanOnce** | **/ScanBoot**
> Specify when to perform the scan and replacement: do it immediately, possibly purging the File Protection cache first, do it at the next boot, or do it at every boot, respectively.

/Cancel
> Cancel all pending scans.

/Quiet
> Suppress confirmation prompts when replacing files.

/Enable
> Enable the Windows File Protection facility, which scans and replaces system files automatically on an ongoing basis.

---

tree

tree *dir* [*options*]

Display the tree structure for the specified directory.

Options

/A
> Use ASCII characters instead of extended graphics characters.

/F
> Include filenames in the display.

Working with Disks and Filesystems

---

chkdsk

chkdsk *x*:[*options*]

Check the filesystem on Drive *x*.

Options

/F [/X]
> Fix any errors encountered. **/X** forces a volume dismount before the check.

/L:*n*
> Change the log file size to *n* KB (on NTFS filesystems only).

/R
> Locate and recover bad sectors.

/V
> Produce verbose output.

dfscmd

dmfcmd [*options*]

Administer the Distributed File System (Dfs) facility on the local system.

Options

/VIEW *dfsroot**share* [/**Partial** | /**Full** | /**Batch** | ^
/**BatchRestore**]

    View the components of the specified Dfs share. /**Partial** adds share comments to the output and /**Full** lists all servers for each volume. The remaining options create batch files suitable for recreating the Dfs, including the /**Restore** switch in the latter case (see the next option, /**MAP**).

/MAP *root**share**path* *server**share**path* [*comment*] ^
[/**Restore**]

    Add a shared folder to the specified Dfs tree. /**Restore** suppresses all checks of the destination server and forces the mapping.

/UNMAP *root**share**path*

    Remove a component from a Dfs tree.

/ADD *root**share**path* *server**share**path* [/**Restore**]

    Add a replica for the specified Dfs tree components. /**Restore** suppresses all checks of the destination server and forces the mapping.

/REMOVE *root**share**path* *server**share**path*

    Remove a replica from the Dfs volume.

dfsutil

dfsutil [*options*]

Administer the Distributed File System (Dfs) facility in a Windows 2000 domain.

Server Options

/LIST:*domain* [/**DCNAME:***name*]

    List the distributed filesystems in the specified domain, using the specified domain controller if included. (This option is necessary if the local system is not a domain controller.)

/VIEW:** *dfsroot\dfsshare* **[/DCNAME: *name*] **[/LEVEL:1]**

Display configuration information for the specified Dfs tree component (share). **/LEVEL:1** requests more detailed output.

/WHATIS: *server*

Display the Dfs server type and Dfs root for the specified server.

/VERIFY: *dfsroot\dfsshare* **[/DCNAME:** *name*]

Verify the metadata for the specified Dfs share.

/DFSALT: *unc-path*

Resolve the specified pathname to the UNC path to the actual data (taking into account replication).

/UNMAP: *dfsroot\dfsshare* **/ROOT:** *server\share*

Remove the share specified in **/ROOT** from the specified Dfs tree.

/REINIT: *server*

Reinitialize Dfs on the specified server.

/CLEAN: *server*

Remove all Dfs-related registry entries from the specified server.

/DCLIST: *domain*

List domain controllers in the specified domain.

/TRUSTS: *domain* **[/ALL] [/DCNAME:** *name*]

List Windows 2000 (or all) domains that trust the specified domain.

Client Options

/PKTINFO

Display information about client Dfs usage on the local system, including local caching of data.

/PKTFLUSH[: *entry*]

Flush the specified Partition Knowledge Table (PKT) entry in the local cache (or all entries if none is specified). Note that the PKT is now a blob.

---

diskcomp

diskcomp *x*: *y*:

Compare the diskettes in Drive *x* and Drive *y* (this may be the same drive).

---

diskcopy

diskcopy *x*: *y*: **[/V]**

Copy the floppy in Drive *x* to Drive *y* (this may be the same diskette drive). **/V** says to verify the copied data.

---

diskmap[RK]

diskmap /D*n*

Display detailed physical geometry data for the specified disk drive (numbering starts at 1).

diskuse[RK]

diskuse [*path*] [*options*]

Display disk space usage by user account for the current or specified directory tree.

Options

/**U:***user*
  Limit the command to the specified user.

/**S**
  Recurse subdirectories.

/**T**
  Format the output as a table.

dmdiag[RK]

dmdiag

Produce an excruciatingly detailed listing of disk information.

format

format *x*: [*options*]

Format the disk partition designated by drive letter *x* (or the diskette in Drive *x:*).

Options

/**FS:***type*
  Specify the filesystem type (NTFS or FAT).

/**V:***label*
  Specify the volume label.

/**A:***n*
  Set the filesystem's allocation unit size to *n* bytes (add the K suffix to designate kilobytes). Valid sizes are powers of 2, from 512 to 64K for NTFS filesystems, and from 8,192 to 16K for FAT filesystems.

The default allocation unit size varies with the partition size: 4K for over 2 GB, 2K for 1 to 2 GB, 1K for 513MB to 1GB, and 512 for 512 MB or less.

/C

Compress files on the new filesystem by default. (This is for NTFS filesystems with an allocation size of 4K or less only.)

/Q

Perform a quick format operation if possible.

/X

Force a volume dismount before formatting.

/T:_tracks,_ **/N:**_sectors_

Specify tracks/side and sectors/track (respectively) for floppy disks.

---

label

label [_x_:] [_label_]

Assign the volume label for Drive _x_ (defaults to the current drive). If no _label_ is specified, you are prompted for it.

---

mountvol

mountvol _dir volume_ | _options_

Mount the specified volume at the indicated directory location.

Options

/D

Unmount a mounted volume (omit the second parameter).

/L

List the volume mounted at the specified location.

---

vol

vol [_x_:]

Display the volume label for Drive _x._

Managing Shares

net share

net share *share-name*[=*path*] [*options*]

Make a directory available to the network or revoke shared access (the =*path* form is used only when defining a new shared resource).

Without arguments, the command lists all currently shared resources. If just a share name is specified (without options), information about that resource is displayed.

Options
/USERS:*n*
> Specify the maximum number of simultaneous users.

/UNLIMITED
> Allow unlimited users to access the share simultaneously.

/REMARK:"*text*"
> Specify a description or other comment for the share.

/DELETE
> Remove the specified shared resource. Either the share name, the path, or the printer device may be specified as the argument to the command.

---

net use

net use [*device*:] [*host**share*] [*password* | *] [*options*]

Map a network resource to a local device, which can be a drive letter or a printer of the form **LPT***n*.

The host and share name argument is used only when defining new mappings. It may have a NetWare volume name appended, if appropriate.

Any required password may be specified on the command line, or an asterisk may be substituted to request a password prompt.

Options
/PERSISTENT:YES | NO
> Create a persistent mapping (automatically re-created at each login). The default is the setting used most recently. If this

---

option is specified without any other arguments, it changes the current default.

/USER:[*domain*]*username*
Specify an alternate user account for accessing the resource.

/HOME
Map the specified drive letter to your home directory (no resource specification is needed).

/DELETE
Permanently remove the specified device mapping.

---

net view

`net view` [*target*]

Display the names of the computers in a domain or network, or display the shared resources on a specified remote system. *target* can be one of the following:

host
The name of a remote system whose shared resources are displayed.

/DOMAIN:*name*
A Windows 2000 domain (its members are listed).

/NETWORK:NW [*host*]
Without a hostname, this option lists all available NetWare servers. If a *host* is included, the NetWare resources for the specified system are listed.

If no *target* is specified, the computers in the local domain are listed.

---

rsm

`rsm` *command* [*options*]

Manage the Removable Storage facility. You can use this command to create media pools, allocate media to them, and perform other related administrative tasks. See the **ntbooks** documentation for details.

Printing

See also **net share** and **net use**.

---

con2prt

con2prt *options* [**/C**[**D**] *hostname**printer-share*]

Add remote printers to the local system. (The command is a script-able version of the Add Printer wizard.)

Options

/C | **/CD** \\ *hostname*\ *printer-share*
> Connect to the specified printer. **/CD** says to make it the local default printer. These options may be specified multiple times; the first **/CD** sets the default printer.

/F
> Delete all existing printer connections.

---

lpq

lpq -S*server* **-P***printer* [**-I**]

Display the status and contents of the specified LPD-based print queue. The final option requests a detailed status report.

---

lpr

lpq -S*server* **-P***printer* [*options*] *file*

Print the specified file to the indicated LPD-based printer.

Options

-C*class*
> Select a banner page based on job class (not supported for all printers).

-J*jobname*
> Specify the job name.

-Ol
> Specify the job type as binary (the default is text). Useful for printing PostScript files in some circumstances.

---

print

print /D:*server**print_share files*

Print text files on the specified remote printer.

Networking-Related Commands

Client Utilities

---

finger

finger [*user*][*@host*]

Display information about the specified local or remote user (the remote host must provide a finger service). If no username is specified, information about all logged-in users is returned.

–L says to use a long listing format (ignored by many systems).

---

ftp

ftp *host* | *IP-address*

Initiate a file transfer session to a remote host, which must provide an ftp service.

Options

–A

    Log on as *anonymous*.

–n

    Suppress automatic initial logon to the remote host.

–w:*size*

    Set transfer buffer size in bytes (the default is 4,096).

–i

    Disable prompting during multifile transfers.

–S:*file*

    Run commands in the specified file instead of starting an interactive session.

–v

    Suppress remote server response messages.

–a

    Use any local interface.

–g

    Disable wildcard interpretation in filenames (known as "globbing").

–d

    Enable debugging messages.

---

hostname

hostname

Display the hostname of the local system.

irftp

irftp *path* [**/H**] | **/S**

Send files over an infrared wireless link. **/S** opens the Wireless Link Properties dialog rather than sending a file. **/H** suppresses the usual Wireless Link dialog when sending the file.

rcp

rcp [**/B**] *files destination*

Copy files to or from a remote system. If the remote system running is Windows-based, it must be running the Remote Shell service. Prepend remote filenames with *host*[.*username*]:.

Options

/H

Include hidden files in the copy operation.

/R

Recurse subdirectories in the file list.

rsh, rexec

rsh *server* [**-l** *username*] *command*
rexec *server* [**-l** *username*] *command*

Execute a command on a remote system using the REXEC or the Remote Shell service, optionally specifying a user account for the remote system.

telnet

telnet *host* | *IP-address*

Initiate an interactive session to a remote host (which must provide a telnet service).

tftp

tftp [**-i**] *host* [**get** | **put**] *file-to-transfer* [*destination*]

Perform a Trivial FTP file transfer. The **-i** option says to perform a binary file transfer (an ASCII transfer is the default). The keywords **get** and **put** specify a local-to-remote and remote-to-local transfer, respectively. The optional final argument specifies an alternate location for the transferred file. Specifying a hyphen as the file to transfer takes input from or sends output to standard input/output as appropriate.

Administrative Utilities

arp

Display and manipulate physical address–IP address translation.

arp /A [*IP-address*] [**/N** *interface-address*]

Display current mappings (limited to the specified IP address and network interface, if present).

arp /S *IP-address physical-address* [*interface-address*]

Specify an address mapping (to the table for specified network interface, if present).

arp /D *IP-address* [*interface-address*]

Delete an address mapping (from the table for specified network interface, if present).

atmadm

atmadm [**-c**] [**-a**] [**-s**]

Display information for the ATM Call Manager facility. The options request information on current connections, network service access point (NSAP) addresses, and the status of each active connection, respectively.

dhcploc[RK]

dhcploc *ip-address* [*dhcp-server-list*]

Locate accessible DHCP servers (authorized and rogue). The command's first argument is the IP address of the local system, or the desired adapter on the local system. The second argument is an optional list of DHCP servers to check, specified by IP address.

Options

/p
Don't display information about servers in the list.

/a:*names* [/i:*seconds*]
Send alerts to the specified names (at the specified interval) whenever a DHCP server that is not in the list is detected.

---

dnscmd

dnscmd [*server*] /main_option *addional-args-and-options*

Administer the Domain Name Service facility. The command's format varies considerably by function. *server* specifies the DNS server upon which to operate (it defaults to the current DNS server). A period may be used to specify the local system. The *main-option* specifies what the command does; the various choices are shown in the following list.

Options

/**Info** [*property*]
Display basic information about the specified DNS server, limiting it to the specified property, if included. See the command help for a list of properties.

/**Statistics** [*filter-mask*] [/**Clear**]
Display DNS server statistics. The display can be filtered by a mask whose components are defined in the command help. /**Clear** zeros all counters for which this is supported.

/**ResetListenAddresses** [*IP-addresses*]
Specify/reset the list of hosts to serve DNS requests.

/**ResetForwarders** [*IP-addresses*] [/**Slave**] [/**Timeout** *tsec*]
Specify/reset the list of DNS forwarders. /**Slave** designates hosts as slave servers, and *tsec* is the timeout period in seconds (the default is 5).

/**EnumZones** [*/type*] [/**Forward** | /**Reverse**]
List zones on a DNS server. The first option limits the list to servers of a specific type; either primary, secondary, cache (caching-only), or auto-created. The second option limits the list to forward- or reverse-lookup zones.

/**EnumRecords** *zone node* [*additional-options*]
List the records for the specified DNS subdomain, where *zone* is the desired zone, and *node* indicates the starting point within

---

it. *node* must be either **@** (the zone root), a fully qualified domain name of a node in the zone (i.e., name with a terminal period), or a simple name that is interpreted as relative to the specified zone. Additional options allow you to limit the types of records returned; see the command help for a complete list.

/Restart
Restart the specified DNS server.

/Config [*zone* | **..AllZones**] *property hex-value*
Set various parameters for the DNS server, either for the specified zone or all zones. See the command help for a list of available properties.

/ClearCache
Clear the cache of the specified DNS server.

/WriteBackFile [*zone*]
Write out all root hints or zone datafiles for a DNS server.

/RecordAdd *zone name* [/**Aging**] [*ttl*] *type data*
Add a record to the specified DNS server for the indicated zone. *type* is the standard DNS record type, *name* is the primary data for the type, and *data* is any additional information needed for the record. For example, for an A record, *name* is the hostname and *data* is the IP address. /**Aging** enables aging for the record (it is off by default). *ttl* is the time-to-live for the record (it defaults to the value in the SOA record).

/RecordDelete *zone type data* [/**F**]
Delete the specified DNS record. /**F** suppresses confirmation prompts.

/NodeDelete *zone node* [/**Tree**] [/**F**]
Delete all DNS records at the specified node. /**F** suppresses confirmation prompts and /**Tree** deletes the entire subdomain rooted at that node.

/ZoneInfo *zone* [*property*]
Display information about the specified DNS zone. The display can be limited to the specified property, if included; see the command help for a list of properties.

/ZoneAdd [*zone*] /**Primary** /**File** *file* [/**Load**] [/**A** *admin*]
/ZoneAdd [*zone*] /**Secondary** *Primary-IPs* [/**File** *file* [/**Load**]]
/ZoneAdd [*zone*] /**DSPrimary**
Create a new DNS zone of the specified type. The /**File** option specifies the zone file to be used and /**Load** says to load existing data from it.

/ZoneDelete *zone* [/**DSDel**] [/**F**]
Delete the specified zone. Include /**DSDel** if the zone is a Directory Services–based primary. /**F** suppresses the confirmation prompt.

/ZoneRefresh *zone*
> Force an immediate refresh for the specified zone on the specified secondary server.

/ZoneReload *zone*
> Reload the specified zone from its database (file or Active Directory) on the specified primary server.

/ZoneUpdateFromDS *zone*
> Update the specified server with zone information from the Active Directory.

/ZoneResetSecondaries *zone* [/**Secure**] [*IP-addresses*]
> Specify/reset the notify list for the specified DNS server. /**Secure** limits access to only the listed secondary servers.

/ZoneWriteBack *zone*
> Write back data to the zone file on the specified DNS server.

/ZonePause *zone*
> Pause the specified zone on the server.

/ZoneResume *zone*
> Resume a paused zone on the specified server.

/ZoneResetType *zone* /**Primary** /**File** *file* [/**A** *admin*] [*options*]
/ZoneResetType *zone* /**Secondary** *Primary-IPs* [/**File** *file*]
/ZoneResetType *zone* /**DSPrimary** [*options*]
> Change the type of the specified DNS server, using options as described under **/ZoneAdd**. Additional options are /**Overwrite_Mem** and /**Overwrite_DS,** which overwrite data from the Active Directory to the active DNS memory, and vice versa, respectively.

/AgeAllRecords *zone node* [/**Tree**] [/**F**]
> Enable aging for records in the specified zone at the indicated node (or throughout the subdomain with /**Tree**). /**F** suppresses confirmation prompts.

/StartScavenging
> Enable scavenging, which searching for and removing stale DNS records by designated servers (disabled by default).

/ZoneResetScavengeServers *zone* [*IP-addresses*]
> Specify/reset a list of servers to perform scavenging.

---

getmac^RK

getmac *server*

Display the MAC address of the selected server (specified in either *server* format or as a fully qualified domain name).

---

iisreset

`iisreset` [*options*]

Manage the Internet Information Services (IIS) facility.

Options

/Restart | **/Start** | **/Stop** | **/Status**
Restart (default), start, stop, or display the status of the IIS facility, respectively.

/Enable | **/Disable**
Enable or disable restarting of IIS.

/RebootOnError [**/Timeout:***s*]
Reboot if a start, stop, or restart operation fails. Optionally, wait *s* seconds for the operation to complete successfully.

/NoForce
Don't terminate IIS server processes if they fail to stop gracefully (forced termination is the default).

ipconfig

`ipconfig` [`/ALL`]

Display the IP configuration for the local system. (**/ALL** requests more detail.)

`ipconfig` `/RENEW` | `/RELEASE` [*adapter*]

Manipulate the DHCP lease, renewing or releasing the system's IP address (or the IP address corresponding to the specified network adapter).

`ipconfig` `/DISPLAYDNS` | `/FLUSHDNS`

Display or flush the contents of the DNS resolver cache.

`ipconfig` `/REGISTERDNS`

Reregister all current DHCP names with the DNS.

ipsecpol[RK]

`ipsecpol` `\\`*server options*

Configure IPSec policies. See W2RKTools.Chm for details on this complex tool.

nbtstat

nbtstat [*options*] [*n*]

Display statistics for NetBIOS over TCP/IP connections, repeating the display every *n* seconds, if specified.

Options

–a *host* | **–A** *IP-address*
  Specify the host of interest by name or IP address.

–c
  Display contents of the remote name cache.

–n
  Display local NetBIOS name definitions.

–r
  Display names resolved by WINS or broadcast.

–S | **–s**
  Display the sessions table, identifying remote systems by IP address or hostname, respectively.

–R
  Purge and reload the remote name cache.

net session

net session [*host*] [**/DELETE**]

Without arguments, display session information for all connections to the local system. If a host is specified, information about the session between the local system and that particular remote system is displayed.

The **/DELETE** option causes the specified session (if a host is specified) or all sessions to terminate, closing all associated open local files.

net statistics

net statistics [**SERVER** | **WORKSTATION**]

Display session-oriented networking statistics. Without an argument, this displays services for which statistics are available. The available keywords request statistics for the server or workstation services, respectively.

netsh

netsh [*context subcommand ...*]

The network subsystem administration utility. This facility, which can function either in interactive mode or as a standalone command utility, provides support for command-line/script-based management of many network facilities, including DCHP (**dhcp** context keyword), network interface (**interface**), routing (**routing**), Remote Access Services (**ras**), and WINS (**wins**). See the **ntbooks** documentation for a plethora of context-specific subcommands and options.

Here are a couple of examples to give you the flavor of using **netsh**:

Specify the primary DNS server for the local system:
> **netsh interface ip set dns "Local Area Connection"** ^
> **static ip-addr**

Add an exclusion range to an existing DHCP scope:
> **netsh dhcp server scope** *name* **add excluderange** ^
> *ip-addr1 ip-addr2*

netstat

netstat [*options*] [*n*]

Display TCP/IP statistics, repeating the output every *n* seconds, if specified. By default, current active connections are listed.

Options

/A
> Include server-side connections.

/E
> Display Ethernet statistics.

/N
> Show numeric IP addresses and port numbers.

/R
> Display the routing table.

/S
> Display per-protocol statistics (specify desired protocol with **/P**).

/P *protocol*
> Specify the network protocol of interest: **TCP**, **UPD**, or **IP**.

nslookup

nslookup [*host*] [*DNS server*]

Perform DNS name translation, using the designated DNS server, if specified. Without options, this command enters interactive mode.

pathping

pathping [*options*] *destination*

Trace routes to the destination, showing the degree of packet loss at each router/link.

Options

/h *hops*
Set the maximum number of hops (the default is 30).

/g *hostlist*
Allow loose source routing for hosts in the list, separable by intermediate gateways.

/p *milliseconds*
Set the wait period between consecutive pings (the default is 250).

/q *num*
Set the number of queries to each computer along the route (the default is 100).

/w *milliseconds*
Set the timeout period to wait for each reply (the default is 3,000).

/n
Don't resolve IP addresses to hostnames.

/T
Attach a layer-2 priority tag to the packets to identify devices that do not support layer-2 priority.

/R
Determine if each device along the route supports the Resource Reservation Setup protocol (RSVP).

ping

ping [*options*] *destinations*

Ping the specified systems, which may be specified by hostname or IP address.

Options

/t | **/n** *count*

Ping continuously until interrupted, or for the specified number of times (the default is 4).

/l *length*

Set the length of the packet in bytes (the default is 32; the maximum is 65,527).

/a

Resolve IP addresses to computer names.

/f

Set the Do Not Fragment flag in the packet.

/i *ttl*

Set the Time to Live parameter.

/v *tos*

Set the Type of Service parameter.

/w

Set the timeout interval in milliseconds.

/r *n* [/s *timestamp*]

Record the route(s) of up to *n* hosts in the Record Route field (*n* can range from 1 to 9); an optional timestamp value can also be specified.

/j | **/k** *hostlist*

Route packets via computers in the specified list, allowing or forbidding them from being separated by intermediate gateways (loose/strict source routed). Up to 9 hosts may be included in the list.

---

pptpclnt, pptpsrv

pptpclnt
pptpsrv *host*

Perform connectivity tests for PPTP connections. Start **pptpsrv** on one system, then attempt to connect to it using **pptpclnt**.

---

qtcp^RK

qtcp -t *receiver-ip-addr*
qtcp -r

Measure network performance via Quality of Service (QoS) tests. These commands start the server and client modes of this utility, respectively. See W2RKTools.Chm for full details.

---

rasdial

rasdial *entryname* [*user password* | * [**/Domain:***domain*]] ^
    [*options*]**rasdial** [*entryname*] **/Disconnect**

Dial a phone book entry using the Remote Access Service (first form) or disconnect an existing connection. An asterisk for the password argument produces a password prompt.

Options

/Phone:*number*
    Dial this phone number.

/PhoneBook:*file*
    Use the indicated phone book file rather than the default (%SystemRoot%\System32\RAS\ *username*.pbk).

/CallBack: *number*
    Specify the callback phone number.

/PrefixSuffix
    Use TAPI location dialing properties when placing the call.

raslist[RK]

raslist

List accessible RAS servers.

rasusers[RK]

rasusers *domain* | *server*

List RAS-enabled user accounts in the specified domain or on the specified server.

route

route [*options*] [*cmd* [*dest*] [**MASK** *netmask*] [*gateway*] ^
    [**METRIC** *hops*]]

View or modify the routing table. *cmd* is one of the following:

PRINT
    Display the specified route, or display all routes.

ADD
    Add the specified route.

DELETE
    Remove the specified route.

CHANGE

Modify the specified route.

The *netmask* defaults to 255.255.255.255; the metric defaults to 1.

Options

/F

Clear all gateway entries from the routing table.

/P

Use with **ADD** to define a persistent route, which survives system reboots.

rpings^{RK}

rpings [**–p** *protocol*]

Start the RPC connectivity test server, limiting testing to the specified protocol, if it's included (e.g., **tcpip**, **namedpipes**, **netbios**, etc.). Use the **rpingc** GUI utility to perform the actual testing.

tracert

tracert *host* | *IP-address*

Display the route to the specified destination.

Options

–h *n*

S et the maximum number of hops used to search for the target computer.

–w *n*

Set the timeout period in milliseconds for each reply.

–d

Do not resolve addresses to hostnames.

winschk^{RK}

winschk

Interactive WINS validation and monitoring utility.

winscl^{RK}

winscl *command*

Administer the WINS service. See W2RKTools.Chm for a list of available commands.

Administering Users and Groups

addusers^{RK}

addusers [*server*] *file*

Manage user accounts on the local or specified server via a prepared file. Options control the command's functioning. See W2RKTools.Chm for the syntax of the input file.

Options

/C [/**P**:*c*]

Create new user accounts and groups. **/P** specifies account flags via one or more of the following code letters: **l** (don't force password change at first login), **c** (user cannot change password), **e** (password never expires), and **d** (account is disabled).

/D

Write user and group data to the specified file.

/E

Delete user accounts as specified in *file*.

/S:*c*

Set the field-separation character for the file. The default character is a comma.

cusrmgr^{RK}

cusrmgr -u *user* [**-m** *system*] [*options*]

Modify characteristics of the specified user account.

Options

–P *password*

Set the user password.

+s | **–s** *flag*

Set or unset account flags, where flag is one of the following: **MustChangePassword**, **CanNotChangePassword**, **Password-NeverExpires**, **AccountDisabled**, **AccountLockout**, or **RASUser**.

–r *newname*

Rename the user account.

–d

Delete the user account.

–c *comment*
    Set the account comment.

–f *fullname*
    Specify the user's full name.

–U *profile*
    Specify the user profile.

–h *dir* **–H** *drive*
    Specify the user home directory or the drive letter mapping.

–n *logon-script*
    Specify the logon script.

–alg *group* | **–agg** *group*
    Add the user to the specified local (**–alg**) or global (**–agg**) group.

–dlg *group* | **–dgg** *group*
    Remove the user from the specified local (**–dlg**) or global (**–dgg**) group.

–rlg | **–rgg** *group newname*
    Rename a local (**–rlf**) or global (**–rgg**) group (**–u** is ignored).

---

delprof[RK]

delprof [*/c:\\server*] [*options*]

Delete inactive user profiles on the local computer or on any specified computer.

Options

/Q
    Suppress confirmation messages.

/D:*days*
    Specify the inactivity period (the default is 0).

---

global[RK]

global *group domain* | *\\host*

List the members of a global group.

---

local[RK]

local *group domain* | *\\host*

List the members of a local group.

---

net accounts

net accounts /sync

Force an update of the user accounts database.

net accounts *options* [**/DOMAIN**]

Modify the system or domain password policy settings. **/DOMAIN** says to operate on the primary domain controller rather than on the local system. (The local system is the default on Windows 2000 server systems.)

Options

/MINPWLEN:*n*

Set the minimum password length to *n* characters (the default value is 0, and the allowed range is 0–14).

/MAXPWAGE:*n*

Set the maximum password lifetime to *n* days (the default value is 42, and the allowed range is 1–49,710). The keyword **UNLIMITED** may be specified for *n* to remove any limit.

/MINPWAGE:*n*

Set the minimum number of days between password changes (the default value is 0, and the allowed range is 0–49,710).

/UNIQUEPW:*n*

Remember *n* previous passwords (the default value is 0, and the maximum value is 24).

/FORCELOGOFF:*mins* | **NO**

Force users to logoff *mins* minutes after their permitted logon times have expired; **NO** disables forced logoffs (this is the default).

net group

Display/modify a global group. For all command forms, **/DOMAIN** says to operate on the primary domain controller rather than the local system. (The local system is the default on Windows 2000 server systems.)

net group

List the global group names in the current domain.

net group *name* [*users*] [**/ADD**] [**/DOMAIN**]

Add a group or add users to an existing group.

net group *name* [*users*] **/DELETE** [**/DOMAIN**]

Delete a group or remove users from a group.

net group *name* [**/ADD**] **/COMMENT:***description* [**/DOMAIN**]

Specify a description for an existing group or for a new group.

net localgroup

Display or modify a local group. For all command forms, **/DOMAIN** says to operate on the primary domain controller rather than on the local system. (The local system is the default on Windows 2000 server systems.) User lists are space separated.

net group

List local group names in the current domain.

net group *name* [*users*] [**/ADD**] [**/DOMAIN**]

Add a group or add users to an existing group.

net group *name* [*users*] **/DELETE** [**/DOMAIN**]

Delete a group or remove users from a group.

net group *name* [**/ADD**] **/COMMENT:***description* [**/DOMAIN**]

Specify a description for an existing group or for a new group.

net user

net user *username* [*passwd* | ***] ^
      [**/ADD** [*options*] | **/DELETE**] [**/DOMAIN**]

Create or modify user accounts. As indicated, the username can be followed optionally by a password or by an asterisk to request a password prompt. Without any arguments, the command lists all user accounts in the local domain or on the local workstation.

Options

/ADD | /DELETE

Add or delete the specified user account. The default is to modify an existing account.

/DOMAIN

Operate on the primary domain controller rather than on the local system. (The local system is the default on Windows 2000 server systems.)

/ACTIVE:YES | NO
Enable or disable the account.

/FULLNAME: *text*
The user's full name.

/EXPIRES: *date* **| NEVER**
The account expiration date, if any.

/HOMEDIR: *path*
The home directory location.

/PASSWORDCHG: YES | NO
Whether users can change their password.

/PASSWORDREQ: YES | NO
Whether a password is required for an account.

/PROFILEPATH: *path*
The path to the user profile for this account.

/SCRIPTPATH: *path*
The location of this user's login script.

/TIMES:ALL | *times*
The allowed login hours.

/WORKSTATIONS: *list*
Limit the allowed login locations to these systems (maximum of eight systems).

/COMMENT: *string*, **/USERCOMMENT:** *string*
Descriptive comments for the account.

/COUNTRYCODE: *n*
Operating system country code (0 means the system default).

---

ntrights[RK]

```
ntrights +r | -r right -u user-or-group [-m system] ^
    [-e event-log-entry]
```

Grant (+) or revoke (-) the specified user right to or from the specified user or group. Optionally, specify a system upon which to execute the operation and a string to place into an event log entry.

The user right must be specified by its case-sensitive internal name (see the "user rights" listing later in this book for more information).

---

sdcheck

```
sdcheck server username [options]
```

List ACL information for the specified fully qualified username. (**sdcheck** also has uses provided by other commands.)

Options

-dumpSD | -dumpALL

    Display a user account object's security descriptor alone or along with all the SDs that are inherited from parents, respectively.

-domain: *domain* [**-user:***username* **-password:***password*]

    Specify the domain and user context for a command.

---

showgrps^{RK}

showgrps [[*domain*]*user*]

List the groups in which the specified user is a member.

Option

/A

    Check all known trusted domains as well as the local/specified domain.

---

showmbrs^{RK}

showmbrs *group*

List the members of the specified group. The group name can optionally be preceded by *name*\, where *name* is a domain name or a hostname.

---

showpriv^{RK}

showpriv *right*

Display all holders of the specified user right (specified by its case-sensitive internal name—see the "user rights" listing later in this book for more information).

---

usrstat^{RK}

usrstat *domain*

List the domain users and their most recent login times.

---

usrtogrp^{RK}

usrtogrp *file*

Add users to groups as specified in *file* (see W2RKTools.Chm for format details).

Managing Processes

at

List or schedule delayed and periodic tasks on the specified computer system. (This defaults to the local system.)

Variations

at [*host*]

List currently pending **at** jobs in the Schedule service queue. Note that **at** jobs also appear in the Scheduled Tasks control panel applet, and may be managed from there also.

at [*host*] *job-ID* **/DELETE**
at [*host*] **/DELETE** [**/YES**]

Remove a pending job (first form) or all pending jobs (second form; **/YES** preconfirms the action).

at [*host*] *time* [*options*] *command*

Schedule a job for one-time or periodic execution; *time* indicates the time of day at which the command runs.

Job Scheduling Options

/NEXT: *weekday* | *n*
> Run the command on the next occurrence of the specified day of the week or on the nth of the month.

/EVERY: *weekday-and-dates-list*
> Run the command on a regular schedule; i.e., on each day of the week or the date of the month specified in the comma-separated list.

/INTERACTIVE
> Allow desktop input when the command executes.

clearmem[RK]

clearmem [*options*]

Clear and allocate memory.

Option

-m*n*
> Allocate *n* MB of memory (the default is all of the memory).

See W2RKTools.Chm for other options.

---

diskperf

```
diskperf -Y[D | V] | -N[D | V] [\\host]
```

Enable (**-Y**) or disable (**-N**) disk performance counters on the specified system (this defaults to the local system). **D** and **V** refer to the counters for physical and logical devices, respectively—for example, **-YD** enables the counter for physical disks. By default, all counters are enabled. The command takes effect once the system is rebooted.

kill

```
kill [/F] item
```

Terminate one or more processes, where *item* is a process ID or a regular expression designed to match a complete task/command name or window title. The **/F** option kills some processes that survive the normal termination signal.

memsnap

```
memsnap
```

Write a listing of all current processes and their memory usage statistics to the file memsnap.log.

net print

```
net print \\host\shared-printer
```

List the contents of the specified print queue.

```
net print [\\host] job-number [/HOLD | /RELEASE | /DELETE]
```

List/manage the specified print job, performing the operation indicated by any specified option.

pmon

```
pmon
```

Continuously display a list of currently running processes, as well as the overall system memory and paging statistics.

ps.vbs[RK]

[cscript] ps.vbs [**/S** server] [**/U** user] [**/W** password]

List the running processes on the local/specified server, showing the complete path to the running executable file. Use the latter two options to specify a user account for authentication purposes.

ptree[RK]

ptree [**-c** server]

Display the process tree on the local or specified server, showing process relationships.

ptree [**-c** server] **-k** | **-kt** pid

Delete the specified process, or delete the process and its entire subtree.

This command requires the Ptree service to be run on the target system. It is automatically installed when the Ptree package is.

pulist[RK]

pulist [\\server] [\\server . . .]

List processes by owner on the specified system(s), defaulting to the local system.

rkill[RK]

List/manage remote processes. This command requires that the Remote Kill service is run on the remote system (also found in the Resource Kit).

rkill /VIEW \\host

List the processes running on the specified remote host.

rkill /KILL \\host pid

Terminate the specified remote process.

rkill /Nkill \\host executable

Terminate the processes running the specified executable.

rkill install | deinstall *host*

Install or remove the Remote Kill service on the specified host.

---

runas

runas /user:*username command*

Execute a command as the specified user.

Options

/Env
> Use the current network environment rather than the specified user's environment.

/NetOnly
> Use the user information for remote access only.

/Profile
> Load the user profile of the specified user.

---

soon^{RK}

soon [*host*] [*seconds*] [/INTERACTIVE] *command*

Run a command after a delay period. This command serves as an alternate interface to the Schedule service on the local computer or on a remote host (see also the **at** command).

soon schedules the specified command to run in the indicated number of seconds (see the following list for defaults). The **/INTER-ACTIVE** option allows it to interact with the keyboard when executed.

soon /D [*options*]

Set the default values for various parameters used by the **soon** command, as indicated by the subsequent options.

Default Setting Options

/L:*n*
> Set the default delay period for local jobs to *n* seconds (this is initially 5 seconds).

/R:*n*
> Set the default delay period for remote jobs to *n* seconds (this is initially 15 seconds).

/I:ON | OFF
> Specify whether the **/INTERACTIVE** option is the default or not (this is initially off).

---

start

start [*window-title*] [*options*] *command*

Start a command.

Options

/D*dir*

    Set the current working directory for the command.

/B

    Start the command as a background process—don't create a new window.

/LOW | **/NORMAL** | **/HIGH** | **/REALTIME**

    Specify the priority class for the new process.

/WAIT

    Start the command and wait for it to complete.

/MIN | **/MAX**

    Start the command and minimize or maximize the new window (respectively).

/I

    Pass the original environment to the command rather than to the current environment.

timethis[RK]

timethis *command*

Run the specified command and report on its execution timing data. It is often useful to combine this command with **start /B** to time a background command.

tlist

tlist [**/T**]

List the current processes in tree format, indicating process parentage hierarchy if **/T** is included.

tlist *pid* | *regular-expression*

List the module information for the specified process or for all matching processes.

typeperf^{RK}

typeperf *interval counters*

Display the current values of the specified performance counters on
the screen, repeating the process every specified interval of seconds.
Performance Monitor counter names are generally specified in the
form *server*]*object**counter* (e.g., \Memory\Available Mbytes).

Managing Services

delsrv^{RK}

delsrv *service*

Delete and unregister the specified service. Use **sclist** to view the
names of installed services.

dumpel^{RK}

dumpel [**-s** *server*] **-f** *output-file* **-l** *log* [*options*]

Write event log entries from the local system or the specified
system to the indicated output file (separating fields by spaces
by default). The **−l** option specifies the event log to dump:
system, **security**, or **application** (the default).

Options

-t

Separate fields by tabs.

−m *source* [**-e** *id-list*] [**-r**]

Specify the source field (i.e., the subsystem) for which to dump
events, further limiting the list to the listed event IDs (up to 10
may be specified) if **−e** is included. The **−r** option reverses the
sense of this filtering, writing all events *except* those that meet
the specified criteria.

-d *n*

Dump events for only the past *n* days.

elogdmp^{RK}

elogdmp *server logtype*

Dump the event log entries from the specified system to standard
output in CSV format. *logtype* is either **Application**, **Security**, or
System.

instsrv *service-name command-path* [*options*]

Install a new service with the specified service name, running the executable indicated by *command-path*.

instsrv *service-name* **remove**

Remove an installed service. Use **sclist** to determine the name of the desired service.

Options

/A *user*
> Run the service as the specified user.

/P *password*
> Specify the password for the user account.

logevent [**-m** *server*] [*options*] *text*

Add an event to the Application event log.

Options

-s *c*
> Specify the event severity level; either **s** (success), **i** (information), **w** (warning), **e** (error), or **f** (failure).

-c *n*
> Specify the event category number (the default is 0).

-e *id*
> Specify the event ID (the default is 1).

-r *string*
> Provide a description of the event's source.

msizap

msizap *items* [**!**]

Remove Windows Installer–related settings and files from the local computer, allowing for a clean reinstallation. *items* consists of one or more code letters that indicate what should be removed. The most important of these are ***** (everything), **F** (Installer-related folders only), **R** (registry keys), **N** (Installer items from the Uninstall registry key), **V** (stop the service), and **A** (change ACLs to Full

Control for Admins only). In addition, the code **T** *prod-code* may be used to limit the action to the specified product.

! says to force a yes answer to any prompts that arise.

net config

net config [SERVER | WORKSTATION] [*options*]

Set configuration information for or display information about the Server and Workstation services.

net config Server Options

/AUTODISCONNECT:*mins*
> Disconnect inactive server sessions after the specified number of minutes. The valid range is –1 (disable) to 65,535 minutes; the default is 15 minutes.

/SRVCOMMENT:*text*
> Add a comment for the server (the maximum length is 48 characters).

/HIDDEN:YES | NO
> If set to **YES**, exclude the server from server lists that are displayed to network users (**NO** is the default).

net config Workstation Options

/CHARCOUNT:*bytes*
> Specify the outgoing buffer size. The valid range is 0–65,535 bytes; the default is 16 bytes.

/CHARTIME:*msec*
> Specify the number of milliseconds to collect data before sending it to a communication device. The valid range is 0–65,535,000 milliseconds (the maximum is ~18 hours), and the default is 250.

Whichever of these options (**CHARCOUNT** or **/CHARTIME**) is satisfied first determines when data is transmitted.

/CHARWAIT:*sec*
> Specify the number of seconds to wait for a communication device to become available. The valid range is 0–65,535 seconds; the default is 3,600 seconds, ro 1 hour.

net continue

net continue *service*

Resume a service that has been paused.

---

net pause

net pause *service*

Pause a running service.

net start

net start [*service*]

Start a Windows 2000 service. Enclose the service name in quotes if it contains internal spaces. Run the command without a parameter to list some available services and their canonical names (see the Windows 2000 help file for a more complete list).

net stop

net stop *service*

Stop the specified service.

netsvc^{RK}

netsvc *service* *host* /*cmd*

Manage services on a remote host. *cmd* is either **list**, **query**, **start**, **stop**, **pause**, or **continue**.

sc^{RK}

sc [*server*] *command service*

Obtain detailed information or manage system services.

Process-related commands (**Start**, **Stop**, **Pause**, and **Continue**) change the state of the specified server's processes.

Query commands such as the following return various pieces of information about the service: **GetDisplayName** (the service's descriptive name), **Qdescription** (the service description), **GetKeyName** (the associated registry key), **EnumDependencies** (list-dependency information), **Query** and **QueryEx** (the current status is basic and detailed), **Qc** (the configuration settings), **Qfailure** (the action taken on process termination), and **SDShow** (show the service descriptor in SDDL format).

Several commands may be used to configure or reconfigure a service: **Create** (add a new service), **Delete** (remove a service), **Config** (change settings), **Description** (set description), **Failure** (specify actions on failure/process termination), and **SDSet** (specify security descriptor).

Finally, the form:

sc boot ok | bad

may be used to specify whether the most recent restart configuration is saved as the last known good configuration.

---

sclist[RK]

sclist [*options*] [*****host*]

List services on the specified host (defaults to the local system).

Options

/R

    Display running services only.

/S

    Display stopped services only.

Accessing the System Registry

---

dureg[RK]

dureg [**/***root-key*] [*key*]

Estimate the size of the entire system registry or of the subtree indicated by the option, which is either **/cr** (HKCR), **/cu** (HKCU), **/u** (HKUS), or **/lm** (HKLM). If *key* is specified, then only the size of the specified key is given.

---

reg

reg *op args* [*options*]

Perform various registry operations. The syntax varies according to the operation specified. Operations are listed, along with their specific syntaxes, following the list of common options. Note that all keys are specified as full paths, beginning with a standard root key abbreviation (HKLM, HKCU, HKCR, or HKCC).

Common Options

/V *value-name* | **/VE**

    Specify a registry value on which to operate. **/VE** refers to an empty (unnamed) value.

/S

Recurse the subtree below the specified key/value.

/F

Suppress confirmation prompts.

Available Operations

reg query [*host*\]*key* [*options*]

Display the value (data) in a registry key. Supports the **/V**, **/VE**, and **/S** options.

reg add [*host*\]*key* [*options*]

Add a specified registry key. Accepts **/V**, **/VE**, and **/F**. Also supports **/T** *type* (specify datatype), **/D** *data* (set value to), and **/S** *char* (specify a separator character for REG_EXPAND_SZ type values; the default is \0).

reg copy [*host*\]*srckey* [*host*\]*destkey* [*options*]

Copy a registry key. Supports **/S** and **/F**.

reg delete [*host*\]*key* [*options*]

Delete a registry key. Supports **/F**, **/V**, **/VE**, and **/VA** (delete all values under the specified value).

reg compare [*host1*\] *key1* [*host2*\]*key2* [*options*] [*output-opt*]

Compare two registry keys. Use **/S** to compare two subtrees. Also supports **/V** and **/VE**. The *output-opt* specifies how differences are reported, and is either **/OA** (all info), **/OD** (only differences), **/OS** (only matches), or **/ON** (no output; use return code for the following results: 0=identical, 2=different, 1= failure).

reg save [*host*\]*key file*

Save the specified key to the indicated file (operation is automatically recursive).

reg restore [*host*\]*key file*

Restore the specified registry key from the data stored in the specified file created with **reg save** (operation is automatically recursive).

reg export *key file* [/**NT4**]

Export a local registry key to a file, using the NT 4 .REG file format if that option is included (operation is automatically recursive).

reg import *file*

Import keys in the specified file into the local registry.

---

reg load [*host*\\]*key file*

Temporarily load keys from *file* (created with **reg save**) into the specified temporary registry key. These keys do not persist across boots.

reg unload [*host*\\]*key*

Unload keys previously loaded at the specified temporary key.

regback^RK

Back up registry hives to disk.

regback *directory*

Back up all registry files to the specified directory, which must *not* already contain registry backup files.

regback *file* MACHINE | USERS *hive*

Back up the specified hive to the specified file, where *hive* is a subtree of HKEY_LOCAL_MACHINE or HKEY_USERS (as indicated by the preceding keyword).

regdmp^RK

regdmp [/m *system* | /h *hivefile hiveroot*]

Dump the local registry (no option), a remote registry (/**m**), or a local registry hive (/**h**). **regdmp** output is suitable to use as input to **regini** (see more on **regini** later in this section).

Option

/s

Produce summary output only.

regfind^RK

regfind [/m *system*] [*options*] *search-string* ∧
    [/r *replace-string*]

Perform search or search-and-replace operations in the local registry or in a remote registry.

Options

/p *keypath*

Begin the search at the specified key location.

/n

Include key and value names in the search. Invalid with /**t**.

/y

Ignore case when searching.

/z [/r]

Include string values that are missing a trailing NULL or that have a length that is not a multiple of the size of a Unicode character. If **/r** is included with **/z**, **regfind** adds the missing NULLs and adjusts the length of the string value (any **replace_ string** is ignored).

/t *datatype*

Limit the operation to data of the specified type (the default is any of the string, _SZ, types).

/b | /B

Look for the search string inside of binary data. **/B** searches in both Unicode and ANSI formats, while **/b** searches only in the former. Any replacement string must be the same length as the search string.

---

regini[RK]

regini *script-file*

Modify the registry according to the instructions in the specified script file. See W2RKTools.Chm for details.

---

regrest[RK]

Restore registry hives that have been backed up with the **regback** command.

regrest *backup-dir save-dir*

Replace current registry hives with the information stored in *backup-dir*, saving the current registry files into *save-dir*.

regrest *backup-file save-file* **MACHINE | USERS** *hive*

Restore the specified registry hive from *backup-file*, saving the current hive to *save-file*. Reboot the system for the new data to become active.

---

scanreg[RK]

scanreg /s *search-string item-options* [*options*]

Search the specified registry entities for the specified character string.

One or more of these must be specified:

/k

    Search key names.

/v

    Search value names.

/d

    Search value settings (data).

Additional Options

/c

    Perform a case-sensitive search.

/e

    Require an exact match.

Active Directory and Domain Management Commands

acldiag

acldiag *object-dn* [*options*]

Display access control information for the Active Directory object (specified by its distinguished name).

Options

/GETEFFECTIVE:*name*

    Display effective rights for the specified user or group. An asterisk for *name* displays the entire ACL.

/TDO

    Generate output in a tab-delimited format.

See the command help for other options.

auditpol[RK]

auditpol [*server*] **/Enable** | **/Disable** [*options*]

Enable or disable security auditing on the local system or on the specified computer.

Option

/*category*:*type*
> Specify events to audit. *category* is either **system**, **logon**, **object**, **privilege**, **policy**, or **sam**. *type* is either **success**, **failure**, **all** (i.e., both), or **none**.

---

browstat

browstat [*options*]

Manage the network browsing infrastructure.

Options

DN
> Display the list of transports bound to the browser. Use this option to determine the canonical name of the transport in which you are interested.

EL *protocol domain*
> Force a master browser election in the specified domain and network transport protocol.

GB *protocol* [*domain*] [**refresh**]
> Retrieve a list of backup browsers in the specified domain for the specified transport protocol.

GM *protocol domain*
> Display a browser master for the specified domain.

GP *transport domain*
> Display a PDC name for the specified domain.

WFW *domain*
> List the Windows for Workgroups computers that are running the browser.

STS [*server*] [**clear**]
> Display browser status for the specified server (defaults to the local system). Adding **clear** says to clear all counters.

STA [**–v**] *workgroup*
> Display browser status for the specified workgroup, with optional verbose output.

TIC *transport domain*
> Stop the master browser for the specified domain.

VW *transport domain* | *server* [**/domain**]
> View the browser list for a specified server or domain. By default, servers are listed; include the **/domain** option to view the domain list instead.

---

csvde, ldifde

csvde [*options*]
ldifde [*options*]

Import/export data to/from the Active Directory via an LDIF (**ldifde**) or comma-separated value (**csvde**) format text file.

Options

/B *user domain password*
Specify the domain and user context for the command.

/I
Perform an import operation (export is the default).

/F *file*
Specify the name of the import or export file.

/S *server*
Specify the system on which to perform the import/export.

/T *port*
Specify the communication port (the default is 389 for LDAP and 3268 for the global catalog).

/D *starting-dn*
Specifty the distinguished name of the starting point for an export operation.

/P *scope*
Set the scope for an export operation: ONELEVEL, BASE, or SUBTREE (the default).

/R *filter*
Set a filter to limit exported data, in standard LDAP format.

/L *attribute-list*
Provide a comma-separated list of attributes to export for matching records.

/O *attribute-list*
Provide a comma-separated list of attributes to exclude from the export.

/M
Omit the Active Directory–specific attributes from an export.

/N
Omit binary values.

/C *old new*
Transform data, changing all instances of the first string to the second string. For example, this can be used to change the domain name or other global data within all records.

/V

A verbose command output.

/J *path*

Set the log file location.

/G

Do not perform paged searches.

/K

Continue processing on errors.

---

dcdiag

dcdiag /S:*server* [*options*]

Test various aspects of the normal functioning of the specified domain controller, including network connectivity, DNS registration, replication success and timeliness, and any similar issues.

Options

/U:*domain\ user* **/P:***password* | *

Specify the authentication credentials. An asterisk for the password causes a password prompt to be issued.

/TEST:*list* | **/SKIP:***list* [**/C**]

Specify which tests to run. **/TEST** indicates a specific list of tests to run, while **/SKIP** indicates a list of tests to skip (all others are performed). In either case, **/C** says to extend the test set to include some optional tests. See the online command help for the complete list of tests.

/A | **/E**

Test all servers in the entire site/enterprise, respectively.

/Q | **/V** [**/I**]

Quiet/verbose mode. **/I** ignores "superfluous error messages."

/F:*file1* **/FERR:***file2*

Specify an output file for output and fatal error output. The files must be different if both are used.

---

dsacls

dsacls *object-dn* [*options*]

Manipulate ACLs on an Active Directory object, which is specified by its distinguished name, and optionally preceded by a specific server name. Without options, the command displays the ACL for the specified object.

Options

/A

Display ownership and auditing data as well as permissions.

/D | **/G** *user-or-group-list*:*permissions*

Deny/grant the specified permissions to the indicated users orto the specified groups. Names are in the form *name@domain* or *domain\ name*.

permissions have a complex syntax (see W2RKSupp.Chm for full details). In their simplest form, they are specified as a concatenated list of two-character permission bit codes, as follows: **GR** (generic read), **GE** (generic execute), **GW** (generic write), **GA** (generic all), **SD** (delete), **DT** (delete tree: object plus children), **RC** (read security data), **WD** (modify security data), **WO** (change ownership), **LC** (list children), **CC** (create child object), **DC** (delete child object), **WS** (write to self), **RP** (read property), **WP** (write property), **CA** (control access), and **LO** (list access).

/R *user-or-group-list*

Remove all entries for the specified users and groups.

/N

Replace the current ACL on the object rather than editing it.

/P [**y** | **n**]

Set the object's protection flag to the specified value (if none is specified, retain the current setting).

/I: *c*

Specify the permission inheritance, which is either **t** (propagate to object and all subjects), **p** (propagate one level only), or **s** (propagate to subobjects only).

/S [**/T**]

Restore the security on the object to the default for its object class, as defined in the schema. **/T** says to recursively restore default security to a tree of objects.

---

dsastat

dsastat /S:*server*;*server*:[*port*] *options*

Compare AD replicas. Options specify the type and scope of the comparison to perform among the servers specified to **/S**. Server names may include an alternate port number (the default is the LDAP port, 389).

Options

/B: *starting-point-dn*

Limit the comparison to the AD subtree rooted at the indicated object, which is specified via its distinguished name.

/Filter: *ldap-filter*

Filter objects in the comparison based on the specified filter given in standard LDAP search syntax; the default is "(object-class=*)".

/Scope: BASE | ONELEVEL | SUBTREE

Set the depth of the tree to compare (specify object only, one level down, and the entire subtree, respectively). The default is SUBTREE.

/T:true | false

If **true**, perform a full-content comparison of the AD trees. By default (which is **false**), compare only object statistics.

/Sort:true | false

If **true**, sort objects by GUID. This speeds up a full-content comparison. (The default is **false**.)

/P: *size*

Set the number of entries to return per query page. The default is 64. Decrease this value for large objects with many specified attributes (e.g., user accounts). The allowed range is 1–999.

/LogLevel: INFO | TRACE | DEBUG

Specify output verbosity (keywords are in increasing order). The default is INFO.

/Output: SCREEN | FILE | BOTH

Send comparison output to the screen, either to a file (named dsastat.log.*nnnn*), or to both locations. The default is SCREEN.

[/U: *user* **[/P:** *password* **]] [/D:** *domain* **]**

Specify a username, password, and/or domain for the command-execution context.

---

dumpfsmos[RK]

dumpfsmos *domain-controller*

Display the names of the domain controllers associated with each of the Flexible Single Master Operation (FSMO) roles.

---

gpolmig[RK]

gpolmig *file* [*options*]

Migrate the Windows NT 4.0 system policy to Windows 2000. The specified file is a saved system policy file (.pol).

Options

/list

Display the Windows NT 4.0 policies in the specified file.

/listgpo

List import-ready Group Policy Objects (GPOs).

/migrate *type name gpo*

Migrate the named policy of the specified type (**user**, **computer**, or **group**) to the specified GPO.

---

gpotool^{RK}

gpotool [**/domain:** *domain*] [**/dc:** *list*] [*options*]

Validate or manipulate Group Policy Objects.

Options

/gpo: *list*

Limit the validation to the comma-separated list of GPOs, specified by GUID or the name selected when they are created.

/new: *names*

Create new GPOs with the specified names.

/del: *names*

Delete the listed GPOs, specified by name.

---

gpresult^{RK}

gpresult [*options*]

Display the effective Group Policy settings (i.e., the RSOP) for the current user and/or for the local system.

Options

/V | **/S**

Request verbose- or super-verbose output. Verbose mode is recommended.

/C | **/U**

Limit the display to computer or user settings.

---

guid2obj^{RK}

guid2obj *guid* [**/server:** *server* | **/site:** *site*]

Display the Active Directory object corresponding to the specified globally-unique identifier (GUID). The options specify a particular server or site to query (the default is the nearest global catalog server).

---

klist[RK]

```
klist tickets | tgt | purge
```

List Kerberos ticket information (current tickets, or the ticket-granting ticket) or purge all cached tickets.

---

ksetup

ksetup *options*

Configure a Windows 2000 client to use an MIT Kerberos server.

Options

[/Domain *domain*] **[/Server** *server*]
> Specify the applicable domain and/or the server name for the command.

/SetRealm *DNS-domain*
> Specify the desired Kerberos realm.

/MapUser *kname name*
> Map the specified Kerberos principal to a local name.

/AddKDC | **/DelKDC** *realm kdcname*
> Add/delete a KDC address for the specified realm.

/AddKPasswd | **/DelKPasswd** *realm server*
> Add/remove a designated Kerberos password server.

/ChangePassword *old new*
> Change the current user's password via **Kpasswd**. Requires **/Domain**.

/SetComputerPassword *passwd*
> Set the password for the local computer.

---

ktpass

```
ktpass /Out file /Princ user /Pass pass | * ^
  /MapUser [/Crypto DES-CBC-MD5]
```

Generate a Kerberos keytab file for MIT Kerberos interoperability (designed to be merged with the existing /etc/krb5.keytab file on the Unix system). The main purpose of this command is to create account mappings for Unix Kerberos-aware services, enabling them to use the Windows 2000 KDC.

The listed options specify the name of the output file as well as the Kerberos principal username and password (use an asterisk to prompt for the password). **/MapUser** says to create the Kerberos principal-to-local-account mapping, associating that user account

---

with the Unix service corresponding to the given Kerberos principal name. The listed **/Crypto** option changes the encryption scheme from CRC to MD5.

The command has additional options and capabilities; see W2RKSupp.Chm for details.

---

movetree

movetree /action **/S** *server* **/Sdn** *source-dn* **/D** *server* ^
    /Ddn *dest-dn*

Move an Active Directory object tree between domains within the same forest. The command indicates that the specified subtree on the specified server is to move to the indicated server and tree location. Servers must be specified with fully qualified domain names.

Action is either **/Check** (preview the move without actually moving), **/Start** (begin the move operation after a preliminary check operation), **/StartNoCheck** (start the move without checking first), or **/Continue** (resume a previous move operation).

See W2RKSupp.Chm for details and restrictions.

Options

/Verbose
    Give more detail in the command output.

/U [*domain*]*user* **/P** *password*
    Run the command in the specified user context.

---

netdiag

netdiag [*options*]

Test various aspects of network connectivity for the local server.

Options

/D: *domain*
    Connect to a domain controller in the specified domain (the default is the local domain).

/TEST: *list* | **/SKIP:** *list* [**/C**]
    Specify which tests to run. **/TEST** takes a specific list of tests to run, while **/SKIP** takes a list of tests to skip (all others are performed). In either case, **/C** says to extend the test set to include some optional tests. See the online command help for the complete list of tests.

/Q | /V | /DEBUG
Quiet/verbose/super-verbose output mode.

/L
Log results to the file NetDiag.Log in the current directory.

/DcAccountEnum
List the domain controller computer accounts.

/FIX
Fix minor problems encountered, as applicable.

---

netdom

netdom *action* [*options*]

Manage Windows NT/2000 domains and trust relationships.

Common Options

/D: *domain* [/**Ud:**[*domain*]*user* /**Pd:** *pwd* | *]
Specify the target domain, and optionally specify a username and password for authentication. (* says to prompt for the password.)

/Uo:[*domain*]*user* /**Po:** *pwd* | *
Specify a username and password for authentication upon the domain specified as the object of the *action* keyword. (* says to prompt for the password.)

/S: *server*
Operate upon the specified domain controller.

/V
Verbose command output.

Available Operations

netdom join *computer* /**D:** *domain* [/**OU:***ou-dn*] [/**Reb:**[*s*]]
Cause the specified computer to join the indicated domain and organizational unit, specified by distinguished name. /**DC** says to make the system a domain controller, and /**Reb** causes a reboot on the affected computer *s* seconds after the operation completes (the default is 20 seconds).

The **add** keyword may be used in place of **join** to create the computer account in the target domain without actually joining. The option /**DC** may be added to create a domain controller account.

netdom move *computer* /**D:** *domain* [/**OU:***ou-dn*] [/**Reb:**[*s*]]
Move the specified computer to join the indicated domain and organizational unit, specified by distinguished name. /**DC** says

---

to make the system a domain controller, and **/Reb** causes a reboot on the affected computer *s* seconds after the operation completes (the default is 20 seconds).

netdom rename *computer* **/D:** *domain* [**/Reb:**[*s*]]

Change the name of a Windows NT 4 BDC computer.

netdom remove *computer* **/D:** *domain* [**/Reb:**[*s*]]

Remove a workstation or member server from a domain (not valid for a domain controller).

netdom verify | **reset** *computer* **/D:** *domain* [**/Reb:**[*s*]]

Verify or reset (respectively) the secure connection between a domain member and a domain controller.

netdom query *item* **/D:** *domain* [**/Verify**] [**/Reset**]

Obtain information about the specified domain. *item* can be either **Workstation**, **Server**, **DC**, **OU**, **Trust** (display list of items of the specified type), **PDC** (display the primary domain controller), or **FSMO** (display FSMO owners). **Trust** accepts the **/Direct** option, which says to limit the list to directly established trust relationships, excluding implied ones.

/Verify says to verify the functioning of the secure channel used for trusts. **/Reset** says to resynchronize that connection.

netdom time [*system*] **/D:** *domain* **/Verify** | **/Reset** [*who*]

Verify/reset (respectively) time synchronization within the specified domain, with respect to the time master. If a specific system is given, then the command is limited to that computer. *who* is either **Workstation** or **Server**, and it indicates whether workstations/standalone servers or domain controllers should be verified or synchronized.

netdom trust *trusting-domain* **/D:** *trusted-domain* [*options*]

Manage trust relationships. Options control the specific actions and are mostly self-explanatory: **/Add**, **/Remove** [/**Force**], **/Verify**, and /**Two-Way**. Trusts can also be established with non-Windows Kerberos domains via the following options: **/Add**, **/Realm**, **/PasswordT:***pwd* (password for new trust), and **/Transitive** (off by default for non-Windows domains). **/Kerberos** can be added to **/Verify** commands to exercise this protocol with non-Windows domains.

---

nltest

`nltest [options]`

Perform various domain administration tasks. This command overlaps with **netdom** considerably. Only its unique, most useful features are listed here; see W2RKSupp.Chm for additional features.

Options

/Server: *system*
Run the command on the specified computer.

/Repl | /Sync
Immediately force a partial or full synchronization of the local system or the domain controller specified to **/Server**.

/SC_Change_Pwd: *domain*
Change the secure channel password for the specified domain.

/DSGetDC: *domain*
Display detailed information about the specified domain controller.

/DSGetSite
Display the name of the current site.

---

search.vbs

`[cscript] search.vbs LDAP://dist-name [options]`

Search the Active Directory. The required argument is the distinguished name of the point at which to begin the search, preceded by LDAP://. (**cscript** is not needed if it is the default WSH engine.)

Options

/C: *criteria*
Specify search criteria (in standard LDAP format). The default is "(ObjectCategory=*)".

/S: *scope*
Set the depth of the search to either BASE, ONELEVEL (the default), or SUBTREE.

/P: *props-to-display*
Display the specified object properties (the default is **AdsPath**).

/U: *user* **/P:** *pwd*
Specify the username and password for authentication.

---

secedit

`secedit /action [options]`

Verify or refresh system security and manipulate security templates. (In this text, we consider only the former functionality; see the **ntbooks** documentation for details.) The */action* option specifies the operation to perform.

---

secedit /RefreshPolicy Machine_Policy | UserPolicy ^
   [/Enforce]

Reapply computer or user security settings to all Group Policy Objects. **/Enforce** forces the refresh even if the settings have not changed.

secedit /Export /Cfg *template-file* [**/Areas** *list*] ^
   [**/MergedPolicy**] [**/Log** *file*] [**/Verbose** | **/Quiet**]

Export security policy settings (merging domain and local policies if **/MergedPolicy** is included) to *template-file*, limiting settings to the space-separated list of specified areas (**SecurityPolicy**, **Group_Mgmt**, **User_Rights**, **RegKeys**, **FileStore**, **Services**), if applicable.

secedit /Analyze /Cfg *template-file* **/DB** *newfile*.**sdb** ^
   /Log *file* [**/Verbose** | **/Quiet**]

Compare current system security settings to those stored in the specified template file, sending the results to the specified log file. In this case, the **/DB** option specifies the name of a new security database file to create and use to perform the analysis; the settings in the specified template file are imported into it for this purpose.

secedit /Configure /Cfg *template-file* **/DB** *file*.**sdb** ^
   [**/Areas** *list*] [**/Overwrite**] [**/Log** *file*] ^
   [**/Verbose** | **/Quiet**]

Apply the template stored in the specified file to the system, limiting settings to the specified areas, if applicable. The database file is again used as the source of the settings to apply; the template file is appended to any existing settings in it (or overwrites it if that option is included) automatically.

secedit /Validate *template-file*

Validate the syntax of the specified template file.

Common Options

/Log *file*
> Specify the location of the command's log file, in which detailed results are written.

/Verbose | **/Quiet**
> Specify extra-detailed or minimal command output. All data is still written to the log file, regardless of these options.

Installation-Related Commands

---

instaler^{RK}, showinst^{RK}, undoinst^{RK}

```
instaler basename setup-command
showinst basename
undoinst
```

instaler performs and monitors an installation procedure. This command records all system changes that result from the specified installation process in the file *basename*.log; this file can be viewed using the **showinst** utility. **instaler** also creates the file *basename*.iml for use by **undoinst** to remove the installed software.

---

netset^{RK}

```
netset answer-file
```

Set various networking parameters, as specified in the answer file. See W2RKTools.Chm for details.

---

sysdiff^{RK}

sysdiff /action arguments

Record or apply system differences.

Options

/Snap *snap-file*
> Record the current computer state for later comparison. After executing this command, perform the operations whose effects you want to record.

/Diff *snap-file diff-file*
> Compare the current system state to the one in *snap-file*, and record the differences in *diff-file*.

/Dump *diff-file text-file*
> List the differences in *diff-file* in the specified text file in a readable form.

/Apply [/M] *diff-file*
> Apply the changes in the specified file to the current system, optionally mapping any user profile files to the default user.

/Inf [/M] *diff-file install-dir*
> Apply the changes in the specified file to the installation directory rooted at *install-dir*, optionally mapping any user profile files to the default user.

---

sysprep [*options*]

Prepare the local system for cloning (i.e., copying to multiple target systems via automated disk duplication). **sysprep** genericizes the system suitable for multiple deployment. See W2RKTools.Chm for details.

Be sure to download the updated version of **sysprep** from the Microsoft web site (Version 1.1 as of this writing).

---

winnt

winnt [*options*]

Install (or upgrade) Windows 2000. This command is most suitable for clean installs. See the Deploy.Chm and Unattend.Doc help files for details on answer files and UDF files.

Use **winnt32** to upgrade from older operating systems; see the **ntbooks** documentation for details.

Options

/**S**:*fullpath*
  Specify the location of the Windows 2000 installation files.

/**T**:*drive*
  Indicate which drive to use for temporary files.

/**U**:*answer-file* [/**UDF**:*id,file*]
  Point to the answer file for an unattended installation, along with the optional Uniqueness Database file and the desired ID that identifies the section to use with the latter file for this installation.

/**R**:*folder* | /**RX**:*folder*
  Specify an optional folder to install, which is retained/deleted after completion, respectively.

/**E**:*command*
  Indicate the command to run at the end of the GUI setup process.

The Windows 2000 Recovery Console

The Recovery Console facility allows Windows 2000 to boot into a limited, console-based mode suitable for repairing damaged systems and configurations. It can be entered by booting from the Windows 2000 distribution CD, and it may be installed on the boot menu with the following command (where *x*: is the CD-ROM drive):

x:\I386\Winnt32.Exe /cmdcons

The Recovery Console supports the following standard Windows 2000 commands: **attrib**, **batch**, **cd**, **chkdsk**, **cls**, **copy**, **delete**, **dir**, **expand**, **format**, **help**, **mkdir**, **rename**, **rmdir**, and **type**. However, few or no options are supported for any of them, and their functioning has been simplified. For example, **copy** can only copy a single file. In addition, the following Recovery Console–specific commands are available:

enable *service-or-driver*[*start-type*]
> Enable/start the specified service or device driver; *start-type* sets the startup attribute for the service/driver, either SERVICE_BOOT_START (start driver at system boot), SERVICE_SYSTEM_START (start driver during power-up boot), SERVICE_AUTO_START (start service at system boot), SERVICE_DEMAND_START (manual service start-up), or SERVICE_DISABLED (service is disabled).

disable *service-or-driver*
> Disable system service or device driver.

diskpart /delete | **/add** *device*
> Manage hard drive partitions, where the options perform the associated action. The device may be specified as a drive letter or as a device name (see the **map** command output for the format).

exit
> Terminate the Recovery Console and reboot the system.

fixboot [*x*:]
> Write a new partition boot sector on the system partition of the specified drive (defaults to the system drive).

fixmbr [*device*]
> Write a new master boot record onto the specified disk (default to the system disk). The device is specified as **\Device\HardDisk***n*.

listsvc

List the available services and device drivers.

logon

Select a Windows 2000 installation to access.

map [*arc*]

Display all drive letters to full device name mappings. If **arc** is included, devices are specified as ARC paths.

systemroot

Set the current directory to the Windows 2000 system directory.

set [*var*[=*value*]]

Set the environment variable values. By default, this command is disabled. To enable it, the following Group Policy setting must be enabled: **Local Computer Policy→Computer Configuration→Windows Settings→Security Settings→Local Policies→Security Options→Recovery Console→Allow copy to floppy** and access to all drives and folders. When this is set to 1, use the **set** command during a Recovery Console session to enable various features by setting the following variables to **true**:

AllowWildCards

Allow wildcards in file specifications.

AllowAllPaths

Access files and directories in nonsystem partitions.

AllowRemovableMedia

Allow file copies to removable media (by default, files can only be copied from such media).

NoCopyPrompt

Suppress file overwrite prompts.

Creating an Emergency Repair Disk

Use the Windows 2000 Backup facility (the **ntbackup** command), and select the **Tools→Create an Emergency Repair Disk** menu path.

Command Equivalents for Program Menu Items

Note: not all items are present on all systems. Daggered items may not be located in the default search path:

Menu Item	Command
Administrative Tools Menu	
Active Directory Domains and Trusts	**domain.msc**
Active Directory Migration Tool	**admtagnt†**
Active Directory Sites and Services	**dssites.msc**
Active Directory Schema Manager	**schmmgmt.msc**
Active Directory Users and Computers	**dsa.msc**
Backup	**ntbackup**
Certification Authority	**certsrv.msc**
Cluster Administration	**cluadmin**
Component Services	**comexp.msc**
Computer Management	**compmgmt**
Configure Your Server	**cmak**
Connection Manager Administration	**cmak†**
Data Sources (ODBC)	**odbcad32**
DHCP	**dhcpmgmt.msc**
Distributed File System	**dfsgui.msc**
DNS	**dnsmgmt.msc**
Domain Controller Security Policy	**dcpol.msc**
Domain Security Policy	**dompol.msc**
Event Viewer	**eventvwr**
Indexing Service	**ciadv.msc**
Internet Authentication Service	**ias.msc**
Internet Services Manager	**iis.msc**
License Manager	**llsmgr**

Menu Item	Command
Local Security Policy	**secpol.msc**
Network Monitor	**netmon**
Performance Monitor	**perfmon**
QoS Admission Control	**acssnap.msc**
Remote Storage	**rsadmin.msc**
Removable Storage	**ntmsmgr.msc**
Routing and Remote Access	**rrasmgmt**
Server Manager	**srvmgr**
Task Manager	**taskmgr**
Telephony	**tapimgmt.msc**
Telnet Server Administration	**tlntadmn**
Terminal Server Manager	**tsadmin**
Terminal Services Client	**mstsc†**
Terminal Services Client Connection Manager	**conman†**
Terminal Services Licensing Manager	**licmgr**
User Manager for Domains (NT4)	**usrmgr**
Windows 2000 Diagnostics	**winmsd**
WINS	**winsmgmt.msc**

Windows 2000 Support Tools Menu

Active Directory Administration Tool	**ldp†**
Active Directory Replication Monitor	**replmon†**
ADSI Edit	**adsiedit†**
Application Compatibility Tool	**apcompat†**
Command Prompt	**cmd**
Dependency Walker	**depends†**
DiskProbe	**dskprobe†**
Global Flags Editor	**gflags†**
Process Viewer	**pviewer†**
Security Administration Tools	**sidwalk.msc†**
SNMP Query Utility	**snmputilg†**
Windiff	**windiff†**

Menu Item	Command
Veritas Software Menu	
VERITAS Discover	**discoz†**
VERITAS Software Console	**seasw†**
Other Useful Commands	
NT4 User Manager for Domains	**usrmgr**
Active Directory Install Wizard (Change Server Role)	**dcpromo**
Open Control Panel Folder	**control**
Registry Editor	**regedt32**
Generic MMC Console	**mmc**
Remote Boot Disk Generator	**rbfg**
IP Security Monitor	**ipsecmon**
Verify System File Signatures	**sigverif**

User Rights and System Privileges

Right/Privilege	Internal Name
Access this computer from a network	SeNetworkLogonRight
Act as part of the operating system	SeTcbPrivilege
Add workstations to a domain	SeMachineAccountPrivilege
Back up files and directories	SeBackupPrivilege
Bypass traverse checking	SeChangeNotifyPrivilege
Change the system time	SeSystemTimePrivilege
Create a pagefile	SeCreatePagefilePrivilege
Create a token object	SeCreateTokenPrivilege
Create permanent shared objects	SeCreatePermanentPrivilege
Debug programs	SeDebugPrivilege
Deny access to this computer from the network	SeDenyNetworkLogonRight
Deny local logon	SeDenyInteractiveLogon-Right
Deny logon as a batch job	SeDenyBatchLogonRight
Deny logon as a service	SeDenyServiceLogonRight

Right/Privilege	Internal Name
Enable computer and user accounts to be trusted for delegation	SeEnableDelegationPrivilege
Force shutdown from a remote system	SeRemoteShutdownPrivilege
Generate security audits	SeAuditPrivilege
Increase quotas	SeIncreaseQuotaPrivilege
Increase scheduling priority	SeIncreaseBasePriorityPrivilege
Load and unload device drivers	SeLoadDriverPrivilege
Lock pages in memory	SeLockMemoryPrivilege
Log on as a batch job	SeBatchLogonRight
Log on as a service	SeServiceLogonRight
Log on locally	SeInteractiveLogonRight
Manage Auditing and Security logs	SeSecurityPrivilege
Modify firmware environment values	SeSystemEnvironmentPrivilege
Profile a single process	SeProfileSingleProcessPrivilege
Profile system performance	SeSystemProfilePrivilege
Remove computer from docking station	SeUndockPrivilege
Replace a process-level token	SeAssignPrimaryTokenPrivilege
Restore files and directories	SeRestorePrivilege
Shut down the system	SeShutdownPrivilege
Synchronize directory service data	SeSynchAgentPrivilege
Take ownership of files or other objects	SeTakeOwnershipPrivilege

Script-Related Constructs

:label

> The named location within the script (target of the **goto** or **call** command).

**%*m*

> The argument number *m*. (Access arguments above the ninth one via the **shift** command.)

%~*cm*

> The modified argument *m*, where *c* can be one or more of the following code letters, which indicate the parts of the argument to use:

f:

> Full pathname.

d:

> Drive letter only.

p:

> Path only.

n:

> Filename only.

x:

> Extension only.

s:

> Use 8.3 names (valid with **n** and **x**).

$PATH:

> Examines the search path in the PATH environment variable and returns the fully qualified pathname for the first match for the argument. Returns an empty string if the item is not found.

%*

> Corresponds to all command parameters.

%*var*%

> Value of variable *var* (local or environment).

errorlevel

> An internal variable set by various commands that often indicates contents of user input (see the discussion of the **if** command in the next section).

Commands Useful in Scripts

call

call *file* | :*label* [*args*]

Run the specified external script file or labeled subroutine within the current script.

choice^{RK}

choice [**/C:***choices*] [**/S**] [**/T:***c,n*] *prompt-string*

Prompt user to select from a list of choices, using the specified string as the prompt text. Sets the ERRORLEVEL variable to the selected choice number (starting at 1).

Options

/C: *choices*
> Specify choice letters (the default is **YN**).

/S
> Make choices case-sensitive.

/T: *c,n*
> Select default choice *c* after a timeout of *n* seconds.

cls

cls

Clear the screen.

echo

echo *message*

Display the specified message text on screen. *message* may not be null. (A string consisting solely of a period at the right margin is the conventional way to create a "blank" output line.)

echo ON | **OFF**

Enable or disable command echoing (it is enabled by default).

exit

exit

Terminate a script immediately, or terminate the current command interpreter if it is executed interactively. (See also **goto :EOF**.)

for

Loop construct.

for [*/D*] %*var*% **in** (*filelist*) **do** *command*

Loop over a list of files. The specified variable is set to each successive item in the file list each time it goes through the loop.

/D says to match directory names in *filelist* only.

for */L* %*var*% **in** (*m,j,n*) **do** *command*

Loop from *m* to *n* by *j*, using the specified variable as the loop index.

forfiles[RK]

forfiles [*selection-options*] [**-c**"*command*"]

Perform a command on each file in a list. (The default action is to display the filename.)

Options

-c"*command*"
Specify the command to execute. The following case-sensitive constructs are available for use within commands:

@FILE	Current filename
@FNAME_WITHOUT_EXT	Bare filename
@EXT	File extension
@PATH	Directory location of fil
@RELPATH	Directory location of file, relative to the current directory
@ISDIR	TRUE/FALSE as appropriate
@FSIZE	File size
@FDATE	File modification date: *yyyymmdd*
@FTIME	File modification time: *hhmmss*

The default command is **cmd /c echo @FILE**.

-p*dir*
Specify the directory location at which to start the search (the default is the current directory).

-m*string*
Select the files matching the specified string, which may contain wildcards (the default is *.*).

−d+ | *−ddmmyyyy* | *n*

Select the files last modified on the specified date, or before (−) or after (+) it. If a number is given instead of a date, select the files modified (−)/not modified (+) within the last *n* days.

−s

Recurse subdirectories.

−v

Verbose output mode.

---

freedisk[RK]

freedisk *x*: *min-bytes*

Set %ErrorLevel% to 1 if the amount of free space on the specified drive is less than the indicated minimum size requirement.

---

gettype[RK]

gettype [*server*] [**/S**]

Set %ErrorLevel% to a value indicating the operating system running on the local/specified system [1=Windows NT Workstation, 2=Windows 2000 Professional, 3=Windows NT Server (non-DC), 4=Windows 2000 Server (non-DC), 5=Windows NT domain controller, 6=Windows 2000 DC, 7=Windows NT Enterprise/Terminal Server (non-DC), 8=Windows NT Enterprise/Terminal Server (DC)].

/S suppresses command output.

---

goto

goto *label*

Jump to the named location in the script.

goto :EOF

Jump to the end of the current script file.

---

if

A conditional command. In all cases, including the **not** keyword, it inverts the logical expression.

if [**not**] *errorlevel n command*

Execute *command* if the value of the ERRORLEVEL variable is/isn't greater than or equal to *n*.

---

if [not] defined *variable command*

Execute *command* if the specified variable is/isn't defined.

if [not] exist *file command*

Execute *command* if the specified file does/doesn't exist.

if [not] [/I] *string1 op string2 command*

Execute *command* if the specified string comparison expression is true/false. The available operators are:

== | *EQU*
  Equal.

NEQ
  Not equal.

LSS
  Less than.

LEQ
  Less than or equal.

GTR
  Greater than.

GEQ
  Greater than or equal.

All operators are case-sensitive. **/I** says to perform a case-insensitive comparison.

---

ifmember[RK]

ifmember *groups*

Set %ErrorLevel% to 1 if the current user is a member of any of the specified groups.

Options
/Verbose
  Display all group membership matches.

/List
  List all groups of which the current user is a member (the group list is ignored).

---

pause

pause

Pause execution until the user presses a key.

---

prompt

prompt *text*

Set the command prompt to *text*, which can contain the following codes, among others (see **prompt /?** for more information):

$D, $T
> Current date, current time.

$G
> Greater than sign (>).

$N
> Current drive letter.

$P
> Current drive and working directory.

$S
> Space.

$_
> Carriage return.

rem

rem *anything*

Comment line, ignored by the command interpreter.

set

Display/set a variable value.

set [*var*]

Display the value of the specified variable (or of all defined variables).

set *var=string*

Set the value of a string variable.

set /A *var=numeric-expression*

Set the variable to the result of the evaluated numeric expression.

setlocal. . .endlocal

setlocal begins a local environment within the script, which is terminated by **endlocal**.

shift

shift [`/n`]

Shift script or command arguments down one place, starting at argument *n* (if specified).

sleep[RK]

sleep *secs*

Pause script execution for the specified time period.

timeout[RK]

timeout *secs*

Wait for the indicated number of seconds; −1 says to wait for a keystroke.

waitfor[RK]

waitfor [`−t` *timeout*] *signalname*

Wait for the specified signal, optionally timing out after the specified number of seconds.

waitfor `-s` *signalname*

Send the specified signal.

Windows 2000 GUI Tips and Tricks

Using the Mouse

Shift-click (on items)
    Select a range of adjacent items.

Control-click (on items)
    Select multiple, but not necessarily adjacent, items.

Shift-click (in window close box)
    Close the window and its parents.

Right-click (on item)

Bring up the item's shortcut menu (this includes its Properties). Pressing Alt-Enter performs the same function for a selected item.

Shift-right-click (on an already selected item)

Include "Open with" selection in the item's shortcut menu.

Alt-double-click (on item)

Open the item's Properties. Pressing Alt-Enter when the item is selected does the same thing.

Control-double-click (on folder)

Reverse the "always open new folder" browsing option setting.

Shift-double-click (on folder)

Open the folder in Explorer view instead of the normal browsing view.

Keyboard Shortcuts

Control-Tab, Control-Shift-Tab

Move between the tabs in a multipanel dialog box, in forward and reverse order, respectively.

Backspace (when browsing)

Move up one directory level.

Ctrl-Esc

Bring up the Start menu.

F3 (desktop only)

Start the Find Files or Folders facility.

Shift-Delete (selected items)

Bypass the Recycle Bin for the currently selected files. You can also make this the default behavior by right-clicking on the Recycle Bin and modifying its Properties.

Win-R

Open the Run dialog box.

Win-F

Open the Find Files or Folders facility.

Win-E
Open Windows Explorer.

Win-M
Minimize all currently open windows.

Win-Shift-M
Undo a Win-M operation.

Win-Break
Open the System Properties dialog box.

Win-U
Open the Accessibility Options Manager.

Win-x
Select the desktop items whose names begin with the specified letter in turn, when that key combination is not already defined.

Useful Windows 2000 Web Sites

Site Lists

* *http://dir.yahoo.com/Computers_and_Internet/Software/ Operating_Systems/Windows/Windows_NT/* and *Windows_ 2000/*

* *http://www.netmation.com/listnt.htm*

Windows 2000 Information

* *http://www.microsoft.com/windows2000/* (this is the official Microsoft site).

* *http://www.ntsecurity.net* (where to find security information, from the Windows 2000 Magazine).

* *http://www.winntmag.com* (this contains information on available hot fixes, plus the latest Windows 2000–related news).

* *http://support.microsoft.com/* (this is the search page for the Microsoft Knowledge Base).

You may also go directly to the article Q*nmopqr* via the following path: *http://support.microsoft.com/support/kb/articles/qnmo/p/qr.htm* (note that *n* may be omitted).

Software Archives

- *http://www.microsoft.com/windows2000/downloads/* (where Service Packs and hot fixes are available).

- *http://www.sysinternals.com* (many advanced utilities are provided here, including some code).

- *32bit.bbs.com* (Beverly Hills Software).

- *http://www.nmrc.org/files/nt* and *snt/* (Nomad Mobile Research Centre; security/hacker-related items are found here).

- *http://www.interlacken.com/winnt/ntrepage.asp?selpage=ntwebsrv* and *ntrepage.asp?selpage=sysadmin* (these are Jim Buyens' Windows Web Server Tools and System Administration Pages).

- *http://www.winsite.com/winnt/* (this is the WinSite security archives).

- *http://www.winportal.com* (this is WinPortal, the original community for Windows 2000 users).

- *www.netadmintools.com* (useful tools for network administration are found here).

Index of Commands

MCSE

Windows 2000 Active Directory

By Alistair G. Lowe-Norris
1st Edition January 2000
642 pages, ISBN 1-56592-638-2

The most important change in Windows 2000 is the inclusion of Active Directory, a fully qualified directory service. It is such an important change that systems administrators are likely to find coming to grips with Active Directory to be one of their biggest headaches. But it doesn't have to be that way. *Windows 2000 Active Directory* gives administrators an in-depth knowledge of AD, and it is an indispensable guide they will turn to whenever they need help.